BRITISH SO
CHINESE ROOTS

Chinese Life in Britain

YUNG YUNG WAH, BURJOR AVARI

&

SIMON BUCKLEY

Countyvise : Liverpool

The Chinese take-away and restaurant have become part of our way of life in Britain, but many of us know very little about the lives of the Chinese who live and work in our society. This book, which contains over 100 photographs and will be of great interest to both schools and the general public, provides a fascinating insight into the lives, culture and origins of the Chinese in Britain.

66 *We would like to thank the Chinese Community of Greater Manchester without whose support and co-operation this book would not have been possible.* **99**

Yung Yung Wah
Burjor Avari
Simon Buckley

First published 1996 by Countyvise Limited, 1 & 3 Grove Road, Rock Ferry, Birkenhead, Wirral, Merseyside L42 3XS in conjunction with members of the Chinese Community.

Copyright © Yung Yung Wah, Burjor Avari and Simon Buckley.

ISBN 0 907768 84 9

Contents

WELCOME

The Chinese Community has established itself as a well-respected, law-abiding and hard working ethnic minority community. But whilst they enjoy a harmonious relationship with the local community, they are often seen as mysterious and belonging to a different culture.

No group is that completely different from other. British or Chinese, we all share the same conviction and belief in basic values, upholding the family and serving the community. The apparent difference is in social behaviour shaped by different culture and heritage.

Most of the Chinese in this country originated from Hong Kong and China, a country with five thousand years of colourful history. It is no easy task to write a book about Chinese heritage and to identify those aspects relevant to the Chinese living in this country. It calls for appreciation of the subject matter and, even more importantly, of the livelihood of the British Chinese.

'British Soil - Chinese Roots' is the fruit of many years of research and refined writing by Burjor Avari and the Buckleys, themselves the best example of integration of two cultures, a partnership of two worlds. Yung Yung has drawn on her extensive knowledge of Chinese culture which is presented in a most enjoyable way. Simon has shown his empathy in his portraits of the Chinese families at work and at play. Together they have presented to the readers an important publication which aims at enhancing mutual understanding and appreciation.

'British Soil - Chinese Roots' is a welcome publication bringing to its readers the wealth of Chinese heritage.

I have enjoyed reading 'British Soil - Chinese Roots'. I hope you do.

Peter K.M. Ma
Senior community Officer
Hong Kong Government Office, London

*B*ritish Soil - Chinese Roots' began as a photographic study of the Chinese Community in Greater Manchester. Initially funded by North West Arts and Oldham Art Gallery, the project forms the centrepiece to a wider photographic study of how the lives and culture of the Chinese people are affected by living in the differing environments of China, Hong Kong and the UK.

'British Soil - Chinese Roots' and a subsequent exhibition 'Hong Kong Beats The Chinese Heart' proved to be very popular with audiences in the UK, Hong Kong and China. This book is really a response to the huge amount of interest in the Chinese people that became apparent during the staging of the exhibitions.

Although the photographs concentrate on the Greater Manchester Chinese Community it is true to say that the subjects covered are relevant to the Chinese throughout the UK.

Simon Buckley

Preface

*D*uring the second half of the 20th century Britain has become an increasingly multicultural country. People from many different places from all over the world, with their own cultures, life styles, customs and religions have settled and made their homes in Britain. They are the new British. They have brought variety and diversity to British society.

Some Chinese began to settle here as early as the beginning of this century, but the majority of them came after the Second World War. They are a people with an ancient culture and civilisation, and they are now establishing themselves as a valued minority ethnic community in their own right. The chinatowns of such cities as London and Manchester bear witness to the scale and importance of their settlement in Britain.

As yet, most people know only a little about the Chinese, about their culture or customs, about what they experience and feel and about how they have learnt to cope and adapt to British life. This book has been written by us to fill this gap. It is meant to provide an understanding of the history, culture and present position of the Chinese in Britain. We have written this book especially for pupils in schools, up to the GCSE level, and for members of the general public. Research for this book has been wide and deep, and has included interviews with a number of British Chinese. The text has been written and revised many times in order to make it extremely readable, and numerous photographs have been included. These photographs form part of a wider exhibition-collection called "British Soil, Chinese Roots", which is the title of this book. The appendices and exercises will be of particular use to school children.

We believe that all of us who live in this country need to know and understand a lot more about the peoples and cultures of Britain. The neighbourhoods of towns and cities that we share with different peoples will become places of peace and harmony if we get to know and respect each other better. Fear and prejudice are mostly caused by ignorance. We hope that this book makes a small contribution to ending fear and prejudice in our society.

Yung Yung Wah Buckley
Burjor Avari
Simon Buckley

Manchester, 1995

人生之旅

THE CYCLE OF LIFE

Chapter One

Introduction to the Chinese World

Our book will concentrate on the Chinese who have come from Hong Kong to live in Britain. Although there are a significant number of Chinese in Britain who are from other parts of South East Asia, by far the majority are from Hong Kong.

However, no matter where the Chinese come from, whether it be Hong Kong, Taiwan, Malaysia or Singapore, they all share the heritage from the vast country of China, their original motherland. The lives of the Chinese are closely affected by their roots in China and so, in order to have any understanding of the Chinese in Britain, or in any part of the world, we must first know something about China, her history, culture and some of her spectacular achievements.

CHINA, A VAST COUNTRY

China is the third largest country in the world, after Russia and Canada. She is so big that nearly 39 United Kingdoms (of Great Britain and Northern Ireland) can be fitted into her land area. Although not the largest country in the world, she is the most populated, with 1.2 billion (ie 1200 million) people. For comparison, the population of Britain is just over 55 million people.

UK

Scale map

As one might imagine, a country the size of China is bound to have a spectacular and varied landscape. With arid deserts, bleak plateaux, broad fertile plains, long and mighty rivers like the Yellow and the Yangtse and a climate that ranges from the sub-arctic in the far north to the tropical and humid in the south, China is a world in itself.

Fields being cultivated in Jiangsu Province, China
▼

China is said to be over-populated, and this is because 90% of the population lives on only one-sixth of the land, that of Eastern China, squeezed between the three fertile valleys of the three great rivers, the Yellow River in the north, the Yangtse in mid-south and west and the Pearl River in the south.

There are huge cities like Beijing, Shanghai and Guangzhou, with populations over 10 million in each of them, while in the intensely cultivated countryside there are more than half a million villages. It was once said that "a Chinese is seldom, in all his life, beyond the earshot of other people".

As well as being famous for growing rice and wheat in huge quantities China produces a wide variety of fruits, crops and vegetables and, with its long and broken coastline, provides many different types of seafoods. Alongside its agriculture are her great industries. Some, like textile, iron and steel, are old and established industries, but there are also many modern micro-chip factories producing ultra modern goods for the millions of Chinese consumers.

Huge amounts of goods and many millions of people are constantly criss-crossing the country by road, train, airline or on canals. China has quite advanced communications systems based on an efficient system of post offices and telephone exchanges. In all the big cities there are facilities for international automatic telex, data transmission, facsimile (or fax) and TV satellite transmissions. But as China looks to the future it continues to keep a firm hold on its long and fascinating history.

THE LONG HISTORY OF CHINA

Bones and tools found in China show that human beings were living there many thousands of years ago. One of the earliest of Stone Age remains is that of a hunter, described by archaeologists as "Sinanthropus Pekinensis" or The Peking Man.

Chinese records suggest that the first dynasty was that of the Xia, between 2200 BC and 1766 BC. It was ruled by a person called Yu, who may be considered more as a mythical character than a historical person. Yu is said to have been so busy struggling with monsters and evil spirits that he did not return to his own palace for thirteen years.

If you look at the Chinese chronology in Appendix 1 you will find that during most of Chinese history over the last 4000 years there have been a series of royal dynasties that have ruled the country. Only since 1912, when China became a republic, has there not been a dynasty.

A threshing machine spewing out stalks at rice harvest time in a village near Shanghai, China.

Dynasties came about through victories in many wars, and some dynasties were a lot stronger and lasted significantly longer than others. The early dynasties were those of Shang (1766 BC to 1122 BC), Zhou (122 BC to 221 BC) and the Qin (221 BC to 206 BC). This latter dynasty was short lived but the Emperor, a warrior called Shi Huang Ti, is credited with being the first emperor to unite China. Qin also gives us the name "China".

The most famous middle dynasties were Han (202 BC to AD 220), Sui (AD 589 to AD 618), Tang (AD 618 to AD 907) and the Sung (AD 960 to AD 1279). It was during the time of these dynasties that China made its most amazing technological advances and reached a peak in its art and cultural activities.

The later dynasties were the Yuan (AD 1215 to AD 1368), Ming (1368 to 1644) and the Qing, sometimes also called the Manchu (1644 to 1911). In 1912 a Republic was established under the leadership of Dr Sun Yat Sen. From 1925 onwards China descended into a civil war between the Nationalists led by Chiang Kai Shek and the Communists led by Mao Tse Dong. Between 1931 and 1945 China was also attacked by Japan. In 1949 the Communists won power, and Mao, the most famous leader of Modern China, ruled until his death in 1975. After 1949 the Nationalists escaped to the island of Formosa, off the coast of China. We now know Formosa as Taiwan.

THE CIVILISATION OF CHINA AND THE CHINESE ACHIEVEMENTS

The word "civilisation" means an advanced state of development in any society or group of people. All great civilisations began in and around cities, and the same was true of the Chinese civilisation. Wherever you travel in China you come across evidence of a civilisation which, for centuries, was far more advanced than anywhere else in the world. Ancient cities and towns, magnificent monuments, canals, palaces and temples dating from two or three thousand years ago bear testament to the achievements of the Chinese.

At one stage, during the Tang and the Sung Dynasties, the Chinese were extremely advanced technologically, and they were on the point of having an Industrial Revolution. Famous Chinese inventions include paper, ink, clocks, the compass, the wheelbarrow, gun powder and printing. We had to "re-invent" most of these things in the West many years later.

The Grand Canal - the longest on earth - was dug in the seventh century AD, while China's most famous structure, The Great Wall, measuring some 6000 km in length, was built by Shi Huang Ti, the first great emperor, to keep out the "barbarians", ie all non-Chinese. When Marco Polo returned home to Genoa after his visit to China at the end of the 13th century he was imprisoned, as no one believed him that a country existed that was so far in advance of their own.

China was also very advanced artistically. As early as the Shang Dynasty inscriptions on tortoise shells and bones give us vivid descriptions of events of that time. These were discovered along with carved jade, ivory and bronzes. In 1974 workers accidentally

► **Grand Canal, Suzhou, China.**

▲
The city walls, Xian, China.

discovered an army of 6000 soldiers and 1400 chariots and cavalrymen made from terracotta and clay. These life-sized sculptures were again from the time of the first emperor and the Terracotta Army, as it is now called, has become one of the wonders of the world.

In millions of Chinese homes and in the museums and art galleries around the world you can marvel at the beauty of Chinese objects of art such as paintings from the Sung Dynasty and vases of porcelain (which the Chinese invented) from the Ming Dynasty. (See the chapter on Chinese Art).

We also know much about China's history because the Chinese have been very great record keepers. Famous historians like Szu Ma Chien wrote historical works that provide us today with valuable evidence about the life and culture of the Chinese people in the past. The Chinese had vast libraries containing thousands of books and manuscripts, while we, in the West, were just beginning to understand the use of written materials.

Indeed, for most of her history, China has led the world scientifically, technologically and culturally, and it is only in the past two or three hundred years, as she became much more inward looking, that she has fallen somewhat behind.

THE CULTURE OF THE CHINESE PEOPLE

In the chapters that follow you will be introduced to many different sides of Chinese culture. Here, however, we would like you to remember four general points. Firstly, it is important to remember that Chinese culture is basically a culture built around the idea of a family. This idea is central to the lifestyle of the Chinese people. Confucius, the wise Master who lived nearly 2500 years ago, said that the family is the most perfect and natural unit for happy living. The family must stay united, and its members must learn to live with each other peacefully. Secondly, in Chinese culture, ceremonies, rituals and celebrations are very vital. From very early times they have helped the Chinese people to understand and make sense of their beliefs, philosophies and traditions. Thirdly, the Chinese have a strong regard for their heritage and culture, and they continue to re-inforce images from old paintings, classical stories, opera, history and music in a modern form through books, magazines, TV, video and audio-cassettes. Finally, it is worth mentioning that Chinese culture can also be very inward looking and isolationist. To the Chinese their country, China, is the Middle Kingdom; their emperor was the Son of Heaven; and they considered themselves as Ancestors of the Dragon. Just as the Great Wall was built to keep out the so-called "barbarians" (other foreign people) in the same way it is sometimes difficult for foreigners to truly enter into the spirit of Chinese culture. Over thousands of years the Chinese have kept themselves very much to themselves.

In Britain, too, the Chinese families try to preserve their traditional culture. Although they learn to adapt themselves to the modern British culture, most Chinese in Britain also feel it is worthwhile to hold on to their own traditions and attitudes because they feel that they can cope better in a foreign country and thereby be better able to preserve their identity.

We hope that this book will encourage you to understand and explore further the lives of the Chinese people in Britain and their rich and ancient cultural heritage.

MIDDLE

KINGDOM

The characters meaning 'China', literally Middle Kingdom.

A family watching Chinese opera on TV in China.
▼

▲ Lion in Manchester Chinatown, towering over a passer-by.

HOMETOWN

Chapter Two

Chinese in Britain

The story of how the Chinese people came to live and settle in Britain is a fascinating one. When we talk about the Chinese in Britain we are mostly referring to those who came from Hong Kong. As we stated in Chapter 1, there are Chinese in Britain from places like Mainland China, Malaysia, Singapore and Taiwan; but the Chinese from Hong Kong are in the majority. So let us first get to know Hong Kong.

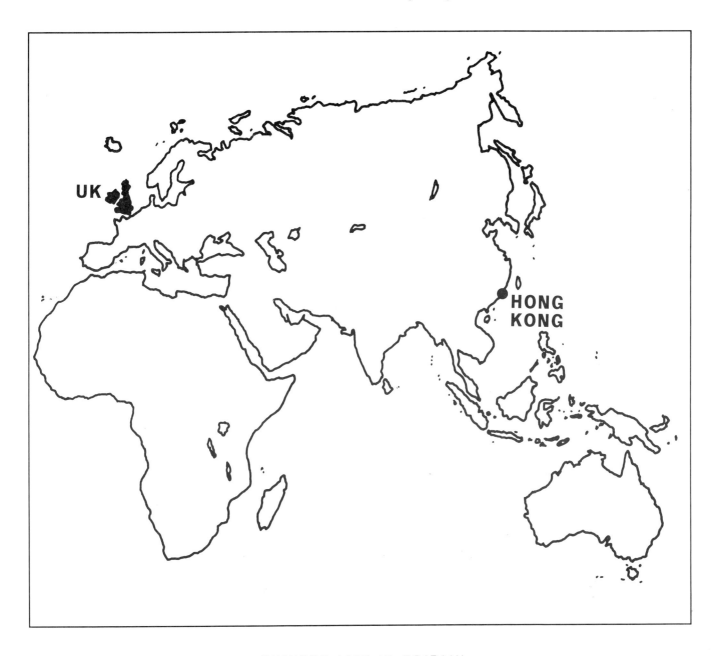

THE STORY OF HONG KONG

Hong Kong, which means Fragrant Harbour in Cantonese, is located on the south coast of mainland China, below the large province of Guangdong. Hong Kong is made up of three areas: Hong Kong Island (about 29 sq. miles), the Kowloon Peninsula (4.6 sq. miles) and the New Territories which consist of a large rural area attached to mainland China and over 200 islands and inlets.

Hong Kong has a population of about six million people, of whom 98% are Chinese. Most of them are Cantonese, ie from Guangdong Province, and so the official language is Cantonese.

China surrendered Hong Kong island to Britain in 1842, after the Opium War. In 1898 the Kowloon peninsula and the New Territories were leased to Britain for 99 years, until the year 1997, when China would regain sovereignty. Britain was anxious to control Hong Kong because it has one of the best natural deep water harbours in the world, making it a major world port of economic and, until recent times, strategic importance.

Causeway Bay, Hong Kong.

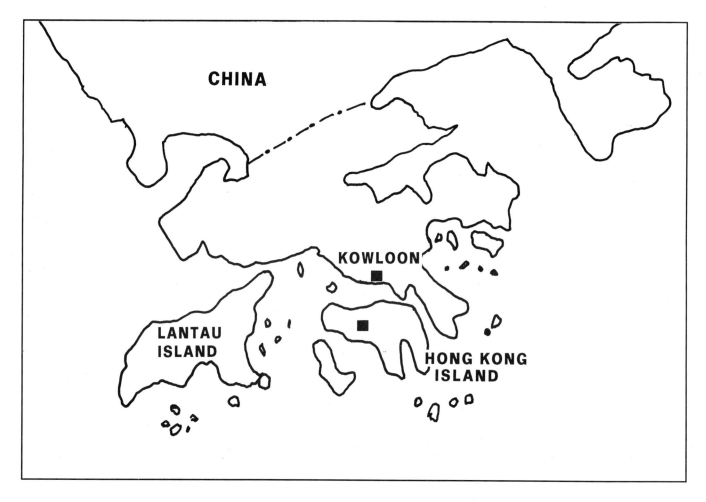

▲
**Victoria Harbour, looking towards
Hong Kong Island.**

Hong Kong Island.
▼

It is on Hong Kong island and the Kowloon Peninsula, connected by ferry and underground road and rail tunnels across the harbour, that we find many of the high rise buildings that we associate with Hong Kong. Urban Hong Kong is a fast and exciting modern city. Here the people are like city people everywhere. They commute to offices, places of work, shops and schools and lead busy lives. The

streets of Hong Kong are often very crowded with people apparently always on the move. The streets below the high-rises are packed with shops and markets selling fresh sea food, meat and vegetables. These shops and markets stay open until late in the evening in order that people may shop after work. It is said that if you try hard enough you will be able to buy anything that you want in Hong Kong. It is one of the world's great economic centres, and billions of pounds' worth of goods are exported and imported via its airport and large container port.

CONNECTIONS WITH CHINA

Despite being under British rule for 150 years Hong Kong retained strong links with China. A great number of Hong Kong's population originally came from China, often from the Guangdong province or Shanghai (on the east coast of China) and many Hong Kong people have relatives in China. Chinese, if asked, will say that they are from the place where their ancestors migrated from. So persons born in Hong Kong but whose parents were from Shanghai,

for instance, would consider themselves Shanghainese.

Everyday thousands of people move between Hong Kong and Guangdong province. China has built a new city, Shenzen, which is also a thriving economic centre, just across the border from Hong Kong. Many people from Hong Kong go there to work and to do business. During the week, therefore, much of the flow of people will be to do with work. Sundays, though, can be just as busy as people go and visit relatives in the towns and villages of Guangdong province.

Many Hong Kong Chinese now buy or build property in Guangdong as well as other parts of China. There is a saying: "Hong Kong is China's gateway, and China is Hong Kong's future".

▲
The British and Chinese flags flying in Manchester Chinatown.

◄
The financial and commercial heart of Hong Kong, known as 'Central'.

THE HAKKAS COME TO BRITAIN

▲
Crops in the New Territories, Hong Kong.

The New Territories, altogether about 270 sq. miles in area, are the more rural part of Hong Kong where the pace of life is much less frantic than in the city. It is from the New Territories that most of the Hong Kong Chinese in Britain have come. These people are called Hakka. Originally from the north of China, the Hakka are the oldest inhabitants of Hong Kong. They have lived in the area for hundreds of years in small village settlements. In each village settlement there is a clan or a family with its own surname, eg. Man, Lee, Lieu, Tang etc.

The Hakkanese are traditionally an agricultural people who had always owned small plots of land on which they grew rice and vegetables. In the 1950's, however, their well-established traditional lifestyle was disrupted when the Hong Kong government bought up many of their ancestral lands in order to build new towns, such as Sha Tin, to cater for the overspill of the urban population from Hong Kong island and Kowloon. Alongside the high rise flats and apartments, now full of people, were created new businesses with large warehouses. With no farming available, the Hakka people found that there was little alternative to working in warehouses or factories at very low wages.

The Hakkas found this situation very difficult to adjust to. In their villages there was a very rigid social structure. Everyone worked and lived as part of and for that village and so clearly knew who was who and the status of each person. The elders of the village had great status amongst the villagers. This structure and status was lost in the factories.

The Hakkas of the New Territories decided it would be better to migrate to far away places like Britain and pursue opportunities there rather than work in the industries and factories of Hong Kong. Britain was indeed a convenient place for the Hakkanese to emigrate to. As Britain ruled over Hong Kong the Hakkas could claim British citizenship, which would make it easy for them to

Sha Tin New Town.
▼

go to Britain. Also, they already had some contacts with friends and relatives who had gone to Britain before the Second World War. These early immigrants, such valuable contacts, had nearly all been sailors with the British Navy or British merchant fleets, and then might have jumped ship at the British ports of London and Liverpool.

SETTLEMENT AND OCCUPATIONS

Before the war most Chinese in Britain lived and worked in the chinatowns of London and Liverpool. They followed two main occupations: laundry work and running chop suey houses. Laundry work was much appreciated then because there were no laundry machines or launderettes in those days. The laundry business proved to be very popular and therefore profitable. The chop suey houses were not yet very popular with the general public because the British diet was still very traditional.

After the war the situation changed completely. The invention of the new laundry machines and the growth of launderettes in most British cities meant that there was not much profit to be made in traditional laundry work. On the other hand, the British diet went through a major change as the British began to appreciate and demand more foreign food. As Chinese food, like Indian food, became more and more popular, the British Chinese began to make profits in the food industry. It was into the catering trade that most of the Hakkanese from the New Territories who came in the 1950s and 1960s went, using a network of contacts already established in Britain. "Take-away" shops and restaurants became familiar on the streets of Britain, and the harder the Chinese worked the more profits they made.

With these profits came prosperity. Some made enough money to go back to Hong Kong to get married. Others built houses in their villages in the New Territories and retired there. There are now

The emigrant village of "Hok Tau" in the New Territories area of Hong Kong.
▼

some villages in Hong Kong which are called "emigrant" communities. That is to say many of the men are away in Britain or other places overseas working and the village earns its income from the money they send back.

▶ *Mr. & Mrs. Wong buying a take-away shop.*

Mr. Wong and Mr. Wong, both from the same clan village in their Liverpool house. Mr. Wong, on the left of the picture, was a sailor who settled in Liverpool after the war, became a chef, and then opened his own business. ▼

CHINATOWNS

▲ **Gerrard Street, London**

◄ **Faulkner Street in Manchester's Chinatown.**

London has the largest chinatown in Britain. It is close to the fashionable West End and so benefits from the custom of hundreds and thousands of tourists who flock to London throughout the year. All year round the chinatown is packed with Chinese shopping and visiting the restaurants. There are innumerable places to shop from as well as cafes and restaurants serving food from all the different schools and traditions of Chinese cuisine. London is also the first to receive the most up to date fashions and trends from Hong Kong.

Up until the 1970's Liverpool had a flourishing chinatown which was also one of the oldest outside China. When Liverpool's economy declined the chinatown shrank, and Manchester took Liverpool's place as the North West's largest chinatown. However, the economic revival of Liverpool, made possible by European funding, has once again rejuvenated its chinatown's prospects.

Manchester's chinatown is built on a site that in the seventies merely contained bleak and empty Victorian warehouses. A group of Chinese businessmen spotted an opportunity, were able to secure funds from Hong Kong and support from the local city

► **The impressive Imperial Archway in Manchester's Chinatown.**

council, and have now turned the site into the second largest chinatown in Britain. Besides the usual shops and restaurants there is also a fine building that contains flats and apartments for senior citizens' residence who wish to have a Chinese community around them. A splendid imperial archway has been built, with the workers specially brought from China to work on original Chinese designs in stone and wood. The chinatown also contains a Chinese sunday school, an art studio, a publishing centre and a Chinese health unit. The Chinese community of Manchester is the fastest growing in Europe, and the chinatown is the focus for the Chinese throughout the North West region of Britain. During this decade this trend is set to continue, with an increasing number of middle class Chinese coming into Britain. The property market will boom, and there will be substantial financial investments·in the heart of the city.

Other cities such as Leeds, Birmingham, Glasgow and Newcastle-upon-Tyne have also seen chinatowns appearing over recent years.

Today, in the chinatowns of Britain, there are three different groups of Chinese people living and

working. The largest group is that of the Hakka settlers about whom we have already talked (in this chapter). Then there is the smaller and newer group of recent arrivals from Hong Kong Island and Kowloon who are well educated and who are interested in professional occupations such as those of lawyers, accountants or computer operators. Finally there are the British born Chinese. With many of them looking to fresh

▲
Freda Lo works for an English firm of garage mechanics. She brings in Chinese clients.

careers outside of the catering industry, the young Chinese are set to bring a new dimension to the Chinese future in Britain. Many of them are either acquiring further qualifications in a variety of studies or becoming entrepreneurs in their own right. Increasingly the self-employed Chinese run

their own garages, pubs, art and design studios, beauty and fashion parlours and engineering works. Their enterprise gives the British economy a further boost.

◄
This youth follows fashion as well as Buddhism in this Manchester temple!

This restauranteur has introduced this novel element to attract business.
▼

CHEUNG FAMILY

Chapter Three

Case Study –
The Cheung Family

▲
*Mr. & Mrs. Cheung
at home.*

M r Cheung was born in Hong Kong in 1943. From his early teens he decides that he wants to see more of the world and so, at the age of 21, he leaves Kowloon City, where he grew up, and comes to the UK. As Hong Kong has been a British Colony he has no problem gaining an entry permit into the UK.

Mr Cheung has relatives in Halifax and they help him get a work permit as well as his first job as a waiter. He lives in staff quarters, 3 or 4 to a room, above the restaurant. The Yorkshire accent, which he finds difficult to understand, and the regular Friday night fights amongst the customers quickly encourage him to move elsewhere and in 1970 he comes to Manchester. Again he finds work as a waiter through a network of friends and relatives. He earns £7.00 plus tips per week which he saves up "Just in case I have to buy a ticket to leave!"

After a couple of years or so Mr Cheung moves to London and, after having been in the UK for over 10 years, he decides to have a holiday from all the stress and go back to Hong Kong for a while.

Whilst in Hong Kong Mr Cheung meets the future Mrs Cheung, also from Kowloon City. They have known each other as children and, after courting for six months, they get married. Mr Cheung finds it hard to get work in Hong Kong after being away for so long and so decides to return to the UK where he can more easily find work and have a

better standard of living.

Mr Cheung arrives back in the UK on his own. Mrs Cheung, who had no idea that one day she was to emigrate, and is none too bothered about coming to England, arrives 3 months later. They set up home in a London bedsit. Mr Cheung is working as a restaurant manager from 11 - 2 and 6 - midnight and so there is little leisure time and chances for days out.

On his day off Mr Cheung sleeps and perhaps goes to the cinema. Mrs Cheung, who after a

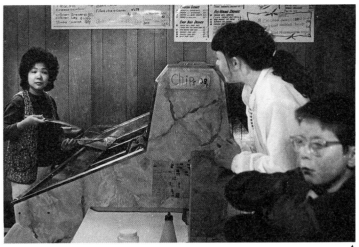

▲
Mrs. Cheung in the take-away.

couple of years is expecting their first child, has very little contact with the outside world, remaining for most of the time inside their room.

Both the Cheung's children, Wai-Ling the daughter and the eldest, and Wai-Hung, their son, are born in London. Wai-Ling lives in London long enough to remember enjoying her early life there. Not only is she surrounded by Chinese culture, going to Sunday school to learn Chinese, she also has plenty of Chinese and English friends to play with and they regularly play at each other's homes. Wai-Hung remembers virtually nothing of his early life in London.

In 1983/4, after Mr Cheung has worked at a restaurant in the Hilton Hotel (better working conditions but poorer pay) the family moves up to Manchester to open their own business, a take-away shop.

The shop is found for them by a friend. Unbeknown to Mr and Mrs Cheung the shop is unfortunately in a rough area of the city. Mr Cheung teaches himself to cook and they copy the menus and prices from other businesses. Mrs Cheung now has to work in the shop as well as looking after the children who, on the whole, have to look after themselves.

Wai-Ling who is now eight, finds moving to Manchester from London difficult to adjust to. She now also has to help in the shop and has left all her friends behind. In London she was able to get out and see things but this is not now possible. The area is too dangerous for her to dare to go out.

◄
The Alsatian that the Cheung's bought to guard their home and shop.

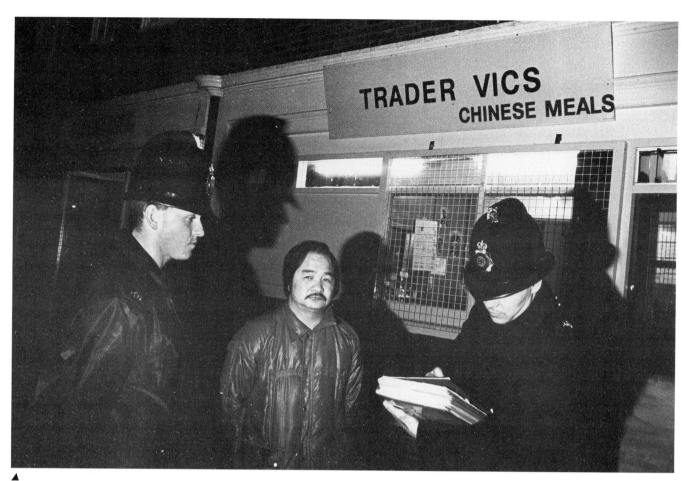

▲
**Mr. Cheung had constant troubles with harassment.
Here he is making a report to the local police**

Wai-Hung in Church.
▼

She also notices that, because of the trouble in the shop, her parents dislike the English much more than she does. They suffer broken windows, racial abuse and vandalism. The police appear powerless to help, leaving Mr and Mrs Cheung feeling isolated. Wai-Hung works in the shop and can understand why his dad keeps an Alsatian. Wai-Ling, though, knows that not all English people are trouble-makers.

Mr and Mrs Cheung suffer the troubles of the business as they, like many Chinese parents, want a good education for their children. The family and its future is their priority. The children are sent to Catholic schools as Mr and Mrs Cheung believe that these schools provide strong discipline and the best academic opportunities. This entails the children becoming Catholics. Mrs Cheung, who is not particularly religious in any way, takes them to church and helps them through baptism. As the children grow to become teenagers their interest in religion wanes somewhat.

Both Wai-Ling and Wai-Hung are the only Chinese at their respective schools but, in their case, they never feel isolated or excluded. In fact their friends

Wai-Hung on his skateboard. ▲

Wai-Hung and Wai-Ling eating at home. ▼

take their being Chinese and able to speak two languages for granted!

With Mr and Mrs Cheung working long hours the children feel the influence of Chinese culture less and less. The Chinese festivals, such as New Year, are celebrated but that is all. As a consequence both children would say that they are Chinese on the outside but British on the inside.

Eventually, after several years, Mr and Mrs Cheung decide that there just isn't enough profit to justify the long working hours and terrible trouble and they sell the shop. They are feeling increasingly isolated, having little time for family and friends.

The children have got used to the routine of working in the take-away after school. The school friends do not need to work after school and Mrs Cheung is always anxious that her children have birthday parties and such like to compensate. As the children enter secondary school they have to cut down on working in the shop because of homework and, soon after, their parents sell the business.

They are keen to retire early and, perhaps, go back to Hong Kong, which they still see as their homeland. They read UK Chinese newspapers to keep in touch with events in Hong Kong. For their children, Hong Kong has not been a major influence as it has for other British Chinese children. The walls of Wai-Ling's and Wai-Hung's bedrooms are filled with posters of English and American stars. They occasionally watch Hong Kong videos but

▲
The Cheung family always try to go out to chinatown together on a Sunday.

both think that their parents wish they were more 'Chinese'.

Mr and Mrs Cheung become anxious that their children should work harder at school to succeed academically in order that they will get good professional jobs. They look back to their own childhoods and the fact that they hardly went out. They struggle to understand the freedoms that their children desire.

Their worries become greater when, after a year or so of unemployment, they buy a restaurant in the Midlands. The large financial overheads and usual troubles from customers put a huge strain on Mr and Mrs Cheung. Mrs Cheung, on top of this, commutes between Manchester

Wai-Hung and his friend playing in the back garden.
▼

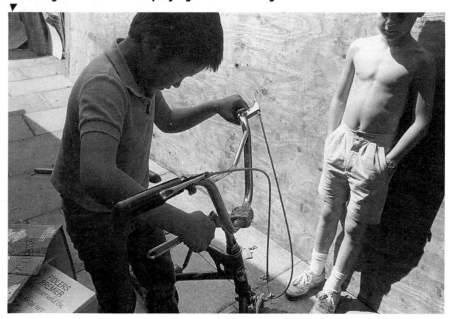

and the restaurant so that she can keep an eye on the children. The children sometimes go and work in the restaurant at weekends to earn pocket money. But the children's increased independence widens the gulf between their parents' Chinese lives and their own principally British lives.

The children have no particular career ambitions. They have both been to Hong Kong in their teens with Mrs Cheung for several months and found it exciting. Wai-Ling might consider working and living there but Wai-Hung wants to live in Britain. Mr and Mrs Cheung have come round to accepting that their children may well marry non-Chinese partners.

Mr and Mrs Cheung have become tired of working six and half days a week and want to retire. "We have become stuck in the UK" says Mr Cheung. "We never wanted to be stuck in the catering trade but with language difficulties it is very difficult to find other jobs. I have a British passport but my face will always be Chinese and so I will never be accepted as British. I have lost my faith in law and order too. One day we will go back to Hong Kong. At least then we'll be able to go to the restaurants each day to "Yam Char"."

If they go it will quite probably mean leaving their children behind. They will most probably find British partners and work in the UK. Behind their Chinese faces they are British.

Mr. & Mrs. Cheung in their restaurant.
▼

LIFE

Chapter Four

Chinese Life Style in Britain

Mr & Mrs. Kwok, who were born in Shanghai, outside their chippy on a Manchester council estate.

The Chinese in Britain, as in other areas of the world, are an incredibly industrious community. In the U.K. the catering trade is by far the most widespread form of business amongst the Chinese, whether it be the small family run take-aways or restaurants which employ a larger number of people.

To make enough money to provide for the family, their children's futures and, quite probably, to send back to relatives in the New Territories the Chinese work extremely hard. The nature of the take-away and restaurant business means very long hours, so that work dominates their lives and life styles.

Here is a typical day in the life of a Chinese family working in a take-away shop:

- **5.00 am to 7.00 am**   Buying fresh meat and vegetables at the wholesale market.

- **7.00 am to 10.00 am**   Sleep and rest.

- **10.00 am to 12.00 noon**   Preparation, which might include peeling and chipping potatoes, chopping vegetables, cutting meat and boiling rice.

- **12.00 noon to 2.00 pm**   Open the shop and serve the customers.

- **2.00 pm to 4.00 pm**   Have lunch, clean up and rest.

- **4.00 pm to 6.00 pm**   Re-open the shop for custom.

- **6.00 pm to 8.00 pm**   Prepare for the evening opening, the busiest opening of the day.

- **8.00 pm to 1.00 am**   Serve the customers.

- **1.00 am to 5.00 am**   Sleep, or perhaps watch Hong Kong and Chinese videos.

This routine is the same everyday except Tuesdays and Sundays. Generally on Tuesdays the take-away is closed, only opening very occasionally at lunchtimes. This day may be spent shopping, whether it be at the cash and carry stocking up on the big bottles of cooking oil, large bags of rice and other provisions needed to feed all those customers, or doing more general household shopping in town. On Sundays the shop only opens in the evening.

Conditions inside the shop can be extremely tiring as it is very busy, and everyone rushes around in the hot and steamy atmosphere to serve the customers as quickly as they can.

To make the business as profitable as possible the whole family works in the shop, which means that there is no need to employ anyone from outside the immediate family. When the children come home from school they will spend some time over their home work, but soon after they will start helping their parents, perhaps by serving at the counter. Used to long working hours, they go to bed quite late.

▶
*Buying vegetables at the
wholesale market.*

For those Chinese who work in restaurants the routine will be somewhat different. The restaurant will normally be open from 11.00 am until well past midnight. There are two shifts, from 11.00 am to 4.00 pm and from 6.00 pm until closing time. The staff will often work both shifts taking a well earned rest for a couple of hours in the afternoon when the restaurant is quiet. In the larger chinatowns, such as London and Manchester, some restaurants remain open until 4.00 am, therefore some staff may start late at about 8.00 pm.

▲
Mr. Chan and a waitress having a meal during a lull in business at his restaurant.

Just as in the take-aways the work in restaurants is very strenuous too. The larger restaurants will employ several chefs and other helpers in the kitchens. When the restaurant is full of diners the kitchen is a place of noise, heat and frantic activity. Through the heat from the large gas cookers and steaming dimsum baskets will come the noise of instructions shouted in Cantonese and the clanking of spatulas in huge woks. Meanwhile waiters whizz in with new orders and out with dishes of freshly cooked Chinese delicacies.

For some workers jobs are not available in their own locality and so they have to travel to work in other towns and cities. Sometimes the workers may stay in staff accommodation at the restaurant during the week. If not, he or she will have to set off mid-morning to get to work and may not return home until 3.00 or 4.00 the following morning. Work like this is very tiring, but to the Chinese men and women in Britain it is nothing strange. They accept it and make the best of it they can.

Meals will be eaten at the place of work during the quiet periods. Take-away owners often live above the shop anyway. The food that is eaten will be cooked on the premises.

Leisure time is very limited. During the working week it is often spent resting or relaxing with videos of the latest Hong Kong TV programmes or Chinese films. The CNE Chinese channel of News and Entertainment, which beams by satellite TV programmes from Hong Kong, is extremely popular; and some of the family programmes and soap operas have become compulsive viewing. Just as the British

may spend their weekends doing DIY, gardening or fixing the car the Chinese will sometimes spend their spare time attending to household needs or they might take the opportunity for a day trip out somewhere, perhaps to the seaside.

The older teenagers, who may have left school, will perhaps, after helping in the shop, go to a disco or, at weekends, to a cinema close to the chinatown which has late night showings of the latest Hong Kong movies. They may also like to eat non-Chinese food such as pizzas or hamburgers and then go for ten pin bowling for their entertainment. The restaurant workers will often do the same.

▲
Mrs. Loong digging the eyes out of the potatoes.

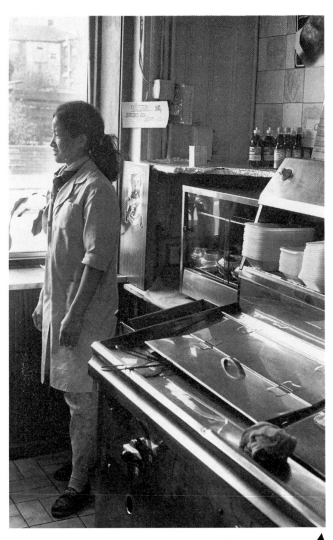

▲
Mrs. Loong in the front of her take-away.

Mr. & Mrs. Loong at the cash and carry which they visit at least once a week.
▼

Mrs. Loong and her brother cooking in the kitchen.
◄

Elaine Loong doing her homework in the shop before helping the family with the tea-time opening.
▼

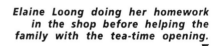

▲
Three of the Loong children playing outside their mother's take-away.

Mr. & Mrs. Loong at a local DIY shop on their day off.
►

SUNDAYS

Sunday is the day when the take-away is closed for the day, and so it has become the most popular day for leisure among the Chinese. This is the same as in Hong Kong where the restaurants are full with diners and the streets jam-packed with people shopping.

In Britain, on Sundays, most of the Chinese take the opportunity to visit their nearest large chinatown.

Families will often travel many miles to visit the chinatown, dressed up in their "Sunday best"!

Top of the list is a visit to a restaurant for dimsum. On a typical Sunday Chinese restaurants have to cater for large numbers of Chinese families and friends. On sunny days and holidays chinatown and its restaurants become almost too crowded to cope! Families and friends cram up to the round tables, sometimes 13 or more to a table, and the restaurant becomes filled with excited chatter as

everybody catches up on the week's news and gossip whilst indulging their favourite pastime of eating. These dimsum meals can last quite a while, and just for that time everybody can believe they are back in Hong Kong.

After the meal there is the chance to buy fresh chicken, eggs, Chinese vegetables and live seafood from the mobile vendors that set up their stalls in chinatowns on Sundays.

Many of the children will attend a Chinese Sunday school for a couple of hours to study the Chinese language (see Chapter 14).

Sunday is also a day when the shops in chinatown do a brisk sale in newspapers and weekly gossip magazines from Hong Kong and China. Through these the Chinese living in Britain not only come to know the latest news from Hong Kong and China but also all about the latest films and TV, along with the Chinese pop and movie stars and current fashions. The video rental businesses in chinatown

◄
Local businessmen taking time to read the Chinese newspapers at the Chinese Chamber of Commerce.

▲
Youths posing in their sports car.

do most of their lending on this day too. Young Chinese will buy CDs and cassettes of their favourite Hong Kong pop stars.

Some of the pop music can be heard booming from the open windows of the flashy cars that some of the affluent youngsters and workers cruise around chinatown in. These cars will have been bought with the money earned from working long hours in the take-aways or restaurants.

Around 4.00 pm the chinatown will quickly become quiet as the families set off home again to open for business.

HOLIDAYS

Because of the pressures of work and business British Chinese do not take holidays very often. Most holidays will be trips to Hong Kong because most relatives and friends live there. The Hong Kong trips will frequently coincide with a major festival such as the Chinese New Year.

It is possible that there may be several years' gap in between the visits to Hong Kong, and so when a visit is made it tends to last at least a couple of months. It is very rarely possible for both parents to travel at the same time, as one has to stay and look after the business. Children generally accompany both parents or, more likely, one of the parents to Hong Kong, and occasionally one or more of the children will fly back without the parents to stay with grandparents, normally during the summer holidays.

Nowadays, during local holidays in Britain, it is becoming more popular to take a short break to somewhere like Spain. And then there are seaside places within Britain which are also frequented by some Chinese families. Those families who cannot afford the time to go away nevertheless try to give their children special treats and a change of scene with perhaps a visit to a theme park or a restaurant selling Western food such as pizzas or burgers, popular with children all over the world!

► **A family on a day out to Blackpool.**

WORK

Chapter Five

A day in the life of Master Chu's Take-Away

▲
**Master Chu cooking in his
take-away kitchen.**

It is 9.30 am on a Friday morning and Master Chu and his wife have just come downstairs from their bedroom in the cold kitchen of their North Manchester take-away for breakfast. It is the start of a day which will not finish until 2.30 am the next morning.

They have been running the 'Double Dragon' for over a decade and so it is a familiar routine. After a breakfast of a fried egg or peanut butter sandwich and mug of tea, it is time to start work.

Mrs Chu begins preparing the food for the day ahead. She will spend most of her day in the kitchen, surrounded by the metal shelves, crowded with bottles of soy sauce, sesame oil, ketchup and brown sauce, alongside jars of cashew nuts, chilli powder, curry paste and other, less immediately identifiable, Chinese ingredients.

Below the framed hygiene certificates rests a large T.V. which, along with her eldest daughter and two sons, will keep Mrs. Chu company throughout the day.

Mrs Chu sets about chopping the ingredients with a practised precision. There have to be enough carrots, spring onions, onions and mushrooms for the lunch, tea and suppertime openings. The neatly sliced vegetables are stored in plastic margarine tubs before she begins the more arduous task of chopping and shredding the beef and pork. It is a job which leaves her arm aching and one on which she spends many hours each working week. Finally she prepares the homemade curry and sweet and sour sauces which have to be made up before each opening.

At 10.30 am, an hour before the lunch opening,

the two sons arrive. The chip range is turned on to warm up (warming the shop too!) and then they prepare the potatoes, firstly peeling them and then, by hand, digging all the 'eyes' out before the potatoes are put through the chipper.

At about 11.00 am, Master Chu sets off to buy provisions. One of the Chinese supermarkets, where he buys his meat and fish, is local but the other is near the City Centre, about 4 miles away. From this one he will have to buy a 100lb sack of rice every week.

Master Chu is so called because he is a kung fu master. Brought up in a Tibetan monastery he has been in Manchester for twenty years. He is a well known figure in the chinatown and for many years has run a kung fu and Chinese medicine centre. He trains the dancers that perform the Dragon dance at Chinese New Year and who also do the lion dancing throughout the year at openings and special occasions.

As the lunchtime opening is the quietest of the day, Master Chu takes the opportunity to open his centre and treat several patients throughout the afternoon.

Master Chu teaching kung fu to an English student at his centre.
▼

Meanwhile back at the shop, after the lunchtime opening and an hour off for lunch and rest, the family are again preparing more chips, meat and sauces. "You have to be very patient" says Tony Chu, the younger son, "there's no time to go out during the day". The big pan on one of the two large stoves is bubbling away, cooking enough rice for the 40 or so portions of boiled rice that may be sold that evening.

At tea-time chips, pies, puddings and fish are the order of the day. The Friday tea-time rush can bring in over 30 customers in one hour and

▲
Master & Mrs. Chu preparing ingredients during the evening opening.

Master Chu's daughter has to frequently heave a big basket of chipped potatoes from the back of the shop up to the counter and tip them into blisteringly hot chip fat.

As tea-time fades into early evening more orders for Chinese dishes come in and Tony makes a much needed cup of 'English' tea for the family.

Master Chu was a restaurant chef for many years before opening the take-away so his food enjoys a good reputation. He uses this to generate extra business by creating his own 'house specials'! Chicken curry boiled rice, Special fried rice (king prawns, chicken, peas, omelette) sweet and sour pork and chow mein (fried noodles) are the dishes which appear most often, as numbers, on the little slips of paper which come from the counter to the kitchen.

As the orders come in Master Chu works quickly and efficiently to get the food ready as soon as possible. Tony takes the phone orders, carefully noting down the address before locating it on the map next to the phone. The food can be delivered to the door in about 25 minutes.

Master Chu carefully measures out the portions of each dish, all committed to memory. A jar lid of cashew nuts, a ladle full of sesame oil, a carton of sauce, a handful of mushrooms -all exact and

repeatable measurements.

The three wooden-handled woks, which have to be replaced once every six months, are rinsed out with a stiff bristled brush. They are all in use as Master Chu deftly dips his ladle into the tubs of vegetable oil, salt and flavourings and tips them into the woks. Once the food is in he turns up the gas, causing a huge burst of flame to leap up under the raised wok in which he tosses and stirs the ingredients. Because of the intense heat the top of the wok range is purposely awash with water to cool the metal down.

After a few minutes the food is cooked and then skilfully tipped into the long foil containers and despatched to the waiting customers.

"Most customers are OK" says Tony, "but some try it on trying to get free food. Sometimes they're drunk and try and tell you they've paid when they haven't! It's up to us sons to sort it out though!" Master Chu rarely ventures to the shop preferring to watch the customers come and go on the small security monitor that he has next to the big T.V. that is, by now, showing a Chinese video film.

At about 8.00 pm Master Chu begins to cook the family's evening meal. It's nothing like the food that his customers buy, being much more traditional

Chinese food. Like tonight, for instance, the family are eating steamed chicken, mince and preserved vegetables, congealed chicken blood and spring onions, salted eggs, and Chinese vegetables.

They sit down to eat at about 8.30 pm when the shop tends to be quieter. However they frequently have to break away from eating to serve customers.

The mid-evening lull means that there are some periods of rest for about 5 or 10 minutes but business continues to trickle in. Phillip Chu, the eldest son, uses the time to chop more ginger and spring onions whilst Mrs Chu begins shredding some more beef. This takes her an hour and by 10.00 she is yawning quite frequently. After that she slices and butters more baps.

Another Chinese film goes in the video just before the late evening rush starts. A phone order comes in every 15 minutes or so and the shop has a constant trail of customers. A lot are regulars who often stick to their favourite recipes "One regular has gone through whole menu, though" says Tony. The sons and daughter pass in and out from the shop to the kitchen and back again, pausing briefly

to see the video for a few seconds.

As the pub shuts the late-evening rush gets properly underway. Although Tony reckons more chips are sold "because they've spent up and can't afford Chinese", Master Chu is still kept very busy. You see the family acting as a well organised team, each knowing their own tasks and watching out for the others. Master Chu is surrounded by clouds of steam from the woks and the constant hiss and spitting and the clanking ladles fills the kitchen with noise.

At 11.45 pm the curry sauce runs out and Phillip hurriedly makes some more. The shop is supposed to close in 15 minutes but they're still working flat out. Finally, at about midnight things quieten down and at 12.30 am the closed sign is finally put up.

Then the clearing up has to begin. All the trays containing the gravy and curry are emptied and cleaned, the scraps are dredged out of the chip fat, the range is wiped down as are all the floors, food

Master Chu and his son Tony pause briefly to catch a glimpse of the TV.
▼

▲
*Master Chu at the end
of the evening.*

is stored away properly, the woks washed and dried and all the other surfaces wiped down.

Eventually after ³/₄ of an hour of constant work by five people, the shop is clean. Work is finished for the day. Master Chu prepares five bowls of steaming hot noodles which the family eat in front of the Chinese film.

Finally at about 2.30 am it is time for bed.

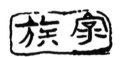

FAMILY STRUCTURE

Chapter Six

Chinese Family Structure

▲
*Mr. & Mrs. Loong with their five children.
The youngest, Andrew, being the son all
Chinese families desire.*

The catering trade and, in particular, the "take away shop", have been the mainstay of successful business for the Chinese in Britain over many years. One of the main reasons for the profitable success of these businesses is the strength of the family unit, the foundations of which were laid down a long time ago in Chinese history. Many of the customs and traditions that we see in a Chinese family have come down to us virtually unchanged over many centuries. It is true to say that the family and its structure form the basis of Chinese society.

HIERARCHY WITHIN THE CHINESE FAMILY

The idea of a hierarchy, or an order of importance and precedence, is a very ancient Chinese idea. It arose from the time when families of whatever size or generation lived in the same house or village. The survival and prosperity of the family depended upon discipline, stability and harmony. Within the family it was important that everyone knew his or her place, in order that the members of the family would be able to live together peacefully. Confucius himself said: "Their families being regulated, their states were rightly governed. Their states being rightly governed, the whole kingdom was made tranquil and happy". Until recent times the family law also took precedence over state law.

Arthur Wong, on the right, is the eldest son and is expected to take on responsibilities within the family

FILIAL PIETY

This is another very important Chinese family ideal. The great philosopher, Mencius, believed that everyone in the family must respect the elder. Through respect one would learn to recognise social responsibilities and to be able to share in a community of high moral and social values. Filial piety teaches that children must obey their parents who brought them out into this world and gave them life. Heaven would punish those who refused to follow the rules of filial piety.

Chinese are brought up to respect their elders.
▼

THE CHAIN OF COMMAND IN THE FAMILY

The great-grandparents or grand parents come at the top of the hierarchy. Even if they are dead a portrait of them would hang from the wall of the sitting room, in order to make clear that they are still with the family in spirit. Their symbolic presence in the house means that they are always available for advice, guidance and protection.

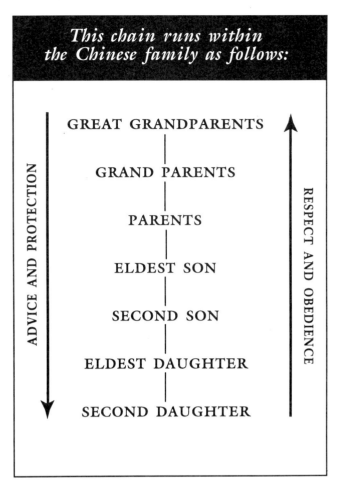

This chain runs within the Chinese family as follows:

ADVICE AND PROTECTION ← | RESPECT AND OBEDIENCE →

GREAT GRANDPARENTS
|
GRAND PARENTS
|
PARENTS
|
ELDEST SON
|
SECOND SON
|
ELDEST DAUGHTER
|
SECOND DAUGHTER

A shrine to ancestors, in the family home, New Territories, Hong Kong.
▼

ANCESTOR WORSHIP

Worshipping dead ancestors is a very common Chinese religious belief, as it is with many other peoples of the world. It is linked with the idea of hierarchy and filial piety. The respect for the elders extends beyond their life time, and this is why ancestor worship developed. Worshipping your ancestors is also meant to bring prosperity and happiness to you and your family. An ancient Chinese hymn expresses this clearly:

Gifts........

> *To their shining ancestors*
> *Piously, making offering,*
> *That they might be vouchsafed long life,*
> *Everlastingly be guarded.*
> *O, a mighty store of blessings!.*
> *Glorious and mighty, these former princes and lords*
> *Who secure us with many blessings,*
> *Through whose bright splendours*
> *We greatly prosper.*

(From A Waley, trans., **Chinese Poems** *(Allen and Unwin 1946).*

TITLES WITHIN THE FAMILY

The hierarchy within the family means that each individual has a title to ensure that all insiders and outsiders are aware of his or her position within the family. The eldest son, for instance, would not be called by his own name by his younger brothers or sisters, but with the title of "Dai-gaw", which means "big brother". The second eldest son would be called "Yi-Gaw", or "second brother".

Blood relationships, too, affect the position within the family, with the titles spelling out clearly which line of descent one is from or referring to. Take grand parents, for example. In Britain we refer to them by one title, (either nana, grandpa, granny or whatever), whether they be on the mother's or the father's side. In the Chinese family, however, a difference is made. The grand mother on the father's side would be called "Yer-Yer", but on the mother's side she would be called "Paw-Paw".

This system of giving exact titles to show position extends right through the family to aunts, uncles, cousins, second cousins etc. The emphasis on "direct descent" blood relations makes it almost like the royal family. There is great pride if five generations still exist.

THE IMPORTANCE OF THE ELDEST SON

When the father dies the eldest son adopts the position of the head of the family, not the mother. The son organises the funeral, and takes on all the financial responsibilities. Inheritance of possessions and, particularly, land also passes to the eldest son in most cases. In the New Territories area of Hong Kong the practice of transferring land to the eldest son still continues. Some women who may have had several daughters continue to try for a son because of this deeply entrenched attitude. This is still the case for many of the Chinese in Britain. (For instance, passing on the family business in the case of restaurant owners).

THE INSTITUTION OF MARRIAGE AND THE NEW BRIDE

Traditionally the Chinese have always regarded the institution of marriage as an important way of strengthening the family unit. Many Chinese marriages even now are arranged, although with greater mobility of people there is a great deal more individual freedom to choose partners. Traditionally the bride is normally taken from another village, so that at first she would be an outsider. Once married she becomes part of the new family; she calls her mother-in-law "mother," and treats her as such. The parents-in-law will meet on special days and at ceremonies, but ordinarily would not mix socially on a day-to-day basis.

In the U.K. "arranged" marriages, or at least introductions, still occur; but this is mostly for those who have reached their early thirties or so and

The Chinese have a saying "The more sons, the more blessings". ▲

◄ A bride at her home with her relative and chief bridesmaid.

remain unmarried. The younger ones make their own choices. Most Chinese in Britain still marry other Chinese but mixed marriages (ie to a partner from a non-Chinese community) are also becoming more prevalent.

Although nowadays it is a remote possibility that people sharing the same surname would be certainly related it is still almost unheard of for two people who share the same surname to marry, just in case! The most common surnames are Chan, Cheung, Lee (Li), Wong, Ho etc. Wong, for example, would not marry another Wong.

◄
A courting couple in Hong Kong.

NAMES

The choosing of a personal name for children is an important part of the family concerns, because the Chinese believe that the choice of name will signal the child's future. For example, a name such as Chan Kam-Choi may be chosen. Chan is the family name, while Kam-Choi, the personal name, means "golden, and with fortune". Girls are given names which evoke beauty or pleasure. For example, Guk Fong would mean "fragrance of the chrysanthemum".

Boy's Chinese name

Girl's Chinese name

A grandmother looks after her grandson whilst the child's parents open the restaurant.
▼

THE CHINESE FAMILY IN BRITAIN

Strong family structure and stability is an important aid to the success of the Chinese in Britain. On first arriving here into an alien culture and environment, the family can provide a framework to build on and also a network to find initial work and accommodation. So, for instance, having a relative working in a Manchester restaurant and therefore being familiar with the Manchester community, could easily lead to a job and a place to live in Manchester.

If only the children have emigrated to Britain to work they will try and re-unite the family as soon as possible, bringing over their parents if they can. If this happens the whole family works together in the business, with the grand parents often acting as childminders.

Family businesses, like restaurants, are passed down from father to son. In Britain, however, some children may not wish to continue with their parents' business. The children, on the whole, are not nowadays forced to take on the responsibility of running the family business if they do not want to. However, if they want to, then Chinese tradition encourages and helps them. The young person who is taking on the task of running the family business will gain respect both from the immediate family and from the wider community. There will be many people who would be willing to help out in any difficulties, because they may wish to repay some of the help they might have received from the young person's parents in

▲
Despite long and inconvenient working hours the family tries to eat their evening meal together.

◄
Mr. Lee owns a hotel. His wife and daughter are involved in the daily running of the business.

the past. In this way the Chinese society continues to function, harmoniously and constructively, century after century.

If the family remains split with one part in Hong Kong and another in Britain, the children will send their earnings back. Some villages in the New Territories rely on this money for their income. In that way the links are maintained. Also, on the death of a parent or a grand parent money will be sent from Britain to buy a large plot of land on which a memorial would be built. This is another way of keeping up the links within the same family.

Despite the considerable strains on the continuation of Chinese lifestyle and traditions that living in modern Britain brings, the family remains of the greatest importance to the Chinese, and loyalty to the family is very noticeable among the Chinese living in Britain.

Chapter Seven

Birth, Marriage and Death - The cycle of Life

▲
Tea ceremony at a wedding in Britain.

Ceremonies concerned with birth, marriage and death are of vital importance to the Chinese. The unique way the Chinese have of celebrating the three great events of life is part of the very fabric of life itself. In China, Hong Kong, Taiwan and Singapore many ceremonies are performed by millions of people as part of their everyday lives. For the Chinese in Britain, too, they are just as important and many are practised, as much as is possible, in the traditional way.

Some of the customs have gradually been changed by Western influences, but strangely this change is often not directly effected by the Chinese in the West, but by fashions that start in Hong Kong, due to Western influences adopted there, and then copied by the Chinese in Britain. Such influences can now be seen in the white wedding dress worn by the bride for part of the wedding and in the sumptuous birthday cakes luxuriously layered with exotic fresh fruits, very popular in Hong Kong, and now available from the U.K. chinatown bakeries.

◄
The character 'Longevity' for sale at a shrine shop in Hong Kong.

WEDDINGS

Before a Chinese wedding can take place a good and auspicious date is chosen from the Chinese calendar. At the wedding ceremony the depictions of the dragon and the phoenix symbolise the bride and groom. Among those Chinese who are Buddhists marriage candles are burnt and ancestors are worshipped at the time of a wedding. A very important ceremony at all weddings is the tea ceremony. Cups of tea are presented to the elders as a mark of respect for them. The elders then present red packets of lucky money. As with birthdays, red is considered as a suitable colour for weddings. Red is associated with wealth and happiness.

Another interesting custom is to send a piece of special marriage cake along with the invitation to the wedding. It is difficult to follow this custom in Britain, so cakes are sent only to close relations and friends. Symbols of fertility are shown at the weddings. These may include special sweets or peanuts which are a symbol of growing and developing together.

The groom's family normally organises a wedding banquet in a restaurant. The banquet consists generally of about ten courses, and the names of all the dishes are related to the idea of marriage. For example the dessert "red bean sweet soup with lotus seed" is chosen because it signifies love and fertility. Other dishes such as Deep Fried Chicken and Roasted Suckling Pig are chosen because their skin becomes reddish in colour and so can signify sending good luck to the couple. Afterwards, firecrackers are exploded as a mark of joy and celebration. With the establishment of large, good quality restaurants in the chinatowns of British cities, Chinese people are able to hold the traditional wedding banquet for many guests. Due to working hours, however, the banquet will nearly always be held in the afternoon when the take-away shops can be closed. Also, because in Britain the bride and groom have to get legally married at the Registry Office, the service at the Registry Office and the Chinese wedding ceremony and banquet may well be held on separate days.

Wedding banquets are often another opportunity for non-Chinese to experience Chinese customs first hand. As the Chinese in Britain make more and more contacts and relationships with the non-Chinese, so these friends are invited to take part in the various ceremonies and festivals.

The bridegroom has his haircut on the eve of the wedding to bring good fortune. Note the whole chicken and candles reflected in the mirror, also to bring good fortune. ▼

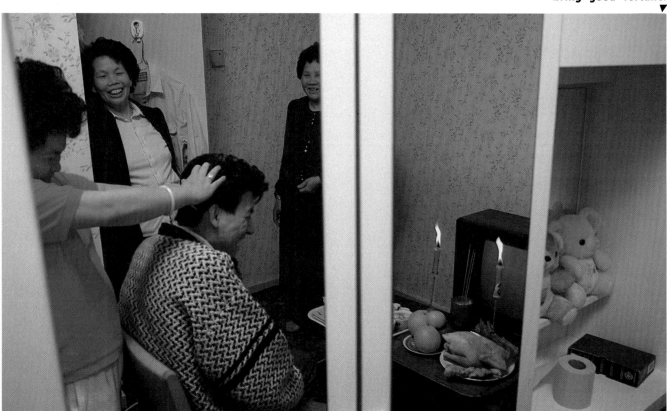

▲
The bride and her bridesmaids leave for the wedding.

▲
The wedding party before the banquet.

Lucky doll on the front of the wedding car. ▶

The bride and her chief-bridesmaid after the banquet in Chinatown.
▼

The bride and groom in their new home.
▼

BIRTHDAYS

Unlike most people in Britain, the traditional Chinese do not celebrate birthdays every year. The birthday ceremonies come in a number of stages. The first birthday in fact comes not at the end of the first year, but at the end of the first month. This is the celebration of "Mun Yut" (ie reaching one month). Until that stage both the mother and the baby do not go out. On the day of the "Mun Yut" friends and relatives send lucky red packets of money or jewellery, because red is an auspicious colour. It is also believed that noodles are a food that grants you long life, so noodles are cooked for this birthday.

After the first month's celebration there are no more birthday ceremonies until the person has reached sixty years! At that age you are considered to have finished the life's cycle, and so when you reach sixty one you are only one year old again. The sixty-first birthday is therefore celebrated, although there is a slight variation in different provinces of China. Grown up children take the responsibility of organising the birthday celebrations.

Everything that is a symbol of longevity, like the Chinese character "Sau", will be on display; and, since a peach is a symbol of long life, peach-shaped buns called Sau Bau are eaten on the birthday.

The next big birthday celebration takes place at the age of seventy one. After that, as a mark of respect, the person's birthday is celebrated every year until death. The birthday of an old person is, in Chinese eyes, more important than that of a young person. Through this example we can clearly see how different Chinese culture can be to Western culture.

The Western influence on Chinese culture, via Hong Kong, is becoming stronger. The Western influence has brought about a big change in the celebration of birthdays in that birthdays have become more of an annual celebration. As well as the cakes and presents many Chinese children in the U.K. have birthday parties just as other British children do. Both the Chinese children and their parents in Britain are increasingly adopting British ways in certain matters, such as the birthday celebrations.

A birthday cake by a Manchester restaurant owner in the popular 'Hong Kong' style. ▼

DEATH

If red is the colour for birthdays and weddings, then white is the colour for death and death ceremonies among the Chinese, particularly if they are Buddhist. At the funeral people are expected to dress from top to bottom in white. Women will wear white flowers as head-dresses. The mourners are given a little, white handkerchief at the ceremony as a symbol of separation. During the funeral incense is burned along with paper money, paper houses and paper motor cars. This is because it is believed that a dead person would have these things in the after life. A vegetarian only "death dinner" is served at the end of the ceremony.

In Britain, the ceremony, for reasons of practicality, cannot be exactly in the same form as in Hong Kong. Although some part of the religious rituals are performed the funeral will still finish with a more standard ceremony at the crematorium or cemetery. In some larger cities, such as Manchester, there is a special area set aside in the graveyard for Chinese people to be buried in.

However, as the Buddhist or Taoist part of the ceremony is very important for many Chinese people they will often arrange for the monks in Hong Kong to hold a ceremony for the deceased. Often the deceased's spouse will go back to Hong Kong for the ceremony and then for as many of the anniversaries as possible. Some of the richer Chinese fly the body back to Hong Kong or build a memorial near their home village. If this is not possible close relatives may well fly back to Hong Kong before the funeral to get the proper funeral and mourning clothes. It is always the eldest son who takes responsibility for these matters.

▲
A paper house for burning at a funeral hangs above a Hong Kong street.

▶
Pictures of dead relatives at a cemetery in Hong Kong.

RELIGION

Chapter Eight

Religions of China and Religious Practices in Britain

Chinese character for "Fortune" on the wall of Mrs. Kwok's take-away. ▶

W hen you are in a Chinese take-away, waiting for your Chinese meal to be cooked, have you ever noticed (after you have read the menu a few times) the posters of elderly, long bearded Chinese men set in highly decorative backgrounds of red and gold? Have you ever wondered who they are, sitting next to the adverts for pies and soft drinks?

These posters are a common sight in Chinese take-aways and of great importance to the Chinese because they are pictorial representations of gods. These gods have been worshipped for thousands of years and are supposed to bring good fortune and health. These gods are from the Buddhist faith, which is the faith followed the most by the Chinese in Britain.

We will talk a little more about the religious practices of the Chinese in Britain, but first let us look at the origins of the religions of China and the Chinese.

RELIGIONS OF CHINA

At the beginning of their history the Chinese came to believe in two important religious ideas. One was the idea that our earth is part of a whole system, the Universe (including Heaven and the Underworld), which is held together by not one God but many gods. The other idea was that the fate of ordinary people on earth is decided by how good they are whilst they are on earth. One way that most people have of keeping the gods happy is by following rituals and practices at the time of great festivals and celebrations.

Chinese religious attitudes have not just been shaped by their beliefs in gods. Nearly 2500 years ago a great philosopher called Confucius established a moral and ethical code for people to follow. He stressed the importance of discipline and harmony within the family which, he taught, would lead to the same discipline and harmony in the nation at large. Just as the father, according to Confucius, was the head of the family, so was the emperor the head of the nation. In a family the father must be obeyed, while in a nation the emperor had to be

Women praying at a temple in China.

obeyed. But both the father and emperor must not abuse their position at the top.

Today many millions of Chinese still follow the teachings of Confucius. Although he is not considered as a god he is worshipped because people have such great respect for his teachings.

Around the same time as Confucius there also lived in China another wise man whose name was Lao Tse. Some of his ideas have come to be known as Taoism. According to Taoism human beings should try to remain in harmony with nature and to avoid behaviour that would upset the natural law of the universe. "It is better to do nothing than to do something unnatural" is one of Lao Tse's key philosophies. The ideas of Taoism are still hugely popular in China and throughout the Chinese world. People who follow Taoism try, through meditation, to achieve peace and harmony with nature. The Taoist teachings are called Tao Te Ching, and there are many Taoist monasteries where people go to worship Lao Tse. Taoism is internationally known through Ying and Yang, which is to do with trying to achieve and maintain a natural balance. The symbol for Ying and Yang is very well recognised as it appears on everything from religious writing to pop record covers.

▲
Muslims at the mosque in Xian, China.

Symbol of Ying and Yang
▶

Confucianism and Taoism developed within China itself. Three other religions came into China from outside. The most popular religion among the Chinese, Buddhism, was introduced from India around the time of Christ by monks travelling along the Silk Road. At first Buddhism was popular only in Northern China, but by the 8th century AD it had spread into Southern China too. Buddhism teaches that human beings will be re-incarnated after death and, therefore, it is wrong to eat animal flesh. Buddhists are vegetarians. Buddhism has had a major influence on Chinese culture, and one of the great Chinese legends, "Journey to the West", tells of a priest's journey to India with his three disciples, the monkey, the pig and the Friar Sand. It is an epic journey full of

battles with evil and the obstacles placed in their path to stop them reaching the West (ie India) where they are to receive the ancient Buddhist scriptures.

In the centuries after Muhammad died in 632 Islam spread to Central Asia and, like Buddhism, entered China via the ancient trade routes. It was the Arab merchants who introduced Islam to China. The Arabs came both by land and by sea. Many millions of Chinese Muslims live in the western parts of China and also in the sea ports of the east. In cities like Xian (ancient Changan) and Guangzhou there are some beautiful mosques.

There is Christianity too in China. Christianity entered China in the 7th century, but did not appear significantly until the 16th century, with the arrival of the Jesuits, the Catholic priests and missionaries. When China was forced to open up to Western trade in the 18th and 19th centuries many missionaries, both Catholic and Protestant, flooded into the country and made many thousands of converts, mainly concentrated in large cities like Beijing and Shanghai. Active mission work declined after the Communists came to power in 1949.

HONG KONG

In Hong Kong, in just about every Chinese home or shop, there is a little shrine to a god. Indeed, in Hong Kong, there are special shops that make and sell only little red wooden shrines. Outside many front doors joss sticks, stuck into oranges, are left burning, filling the high rise apartment blocks with the smell of incense. It is not unusual to see people making offerings in the street, burning paper money or again burning oranges and roast chickens.

On Sundays the big temples in Hong Kong and the New Territories are packed with people praying and making their offerings. Buddhism and Taoism are the main religions in Hong Kong but, with the Western influence and the setting up of academically strong church schools, Christianity is fairly common too.

▲
Wong Tai Sin Temple in Kowloon, Hong Kong is packed at weekends.

◄ **A shrine in a children's clothes shop, New Territories, Hong Kong.**

Mrs Wong worshipping in the garden of her home
whilst her English neighbour washes his car. ▲

RELIGIOUS BELIEFS
AND PRACTICES IN BRITAIN

As the majority of Chinese in Britain are from Hong Kong it is logical that by far the majority follow either the Buddhist faith or Taoism. There are popular deities that are worshipped in Britain, and indeed it is often possible to see either their statue or picture on the walls of take-aways and in Chinese homes.

One such deity is Koom Yam, the goddess of mercy, worshipped by those who wish to have children. Other gods and goddesses such as the God of Land, the God of War and the Monkey God are also given great respect. Kwan Tai or the God of War is particularly popular. The statues of Kwan Tai are placed in martial arts centres, shops or restaurants. In Hong Kong they

are even found in police stations! Kwan Tai is the patron saint of many trades and professions, and he is said to be exercising good and benign influence upon the whole country.

In most Chinese homes three statues are on display, perhaps in a display cabinet or on shelves. They are (and they have to be in this order) the Gods of Luck, Wealth and Longevity, the three important elements of life. Another popular god, particularly so in Britain for obvious reasons, is the Kitchen God, and many rituals are observed on the 23rd day of the 12th moon, a week before the Chinese New Year, in his honour. The God of Land, Tao Tei King, is often located on the

ground floor of a house to keep the household safe. Statues of the Buddha and Koom Yam are placed on shelves and fresh fruits, wine and joss sticks are offered.

Buddhists in Britain raise large sums of money to set up temples here. Perhaps the largest Buddhist temple in Britain is the Samye Ling Tibetan Buddhist temple in Scotland, which attracts many Chinese and Western visitors from all over the country. Birmingham has the second largest temple, and London has many smaller ones. Buddhists organise trips to the U.K. of high ranking monks and priests from Hong Kong, China and Thailand. The Buddhist religion is becoming increasingly popular throughout the Western world.

In Chinese temples there is generally a fortune teller who is supposed to be able to interpret "I Ching" (the famous Book of Changes). The Chinese think of fortune tellers as gifted people who have links with the gods. They will consult them if they wish to fix an auspicious date for marriage, for starting a new business or for moving house.

In connection with one's house there is an interesting Chinese idea which is worth thinking about. This is the idea of Fung Shui (or the force

of wind and water). Before choosing a property and settling in it, many Chinese would consult a Fung Shui expert. This person would indicate whether a particular site or location is good enough for the house. For example, a house facing the sea but with hills behind it is more preferable than the other way round. This example, however, is a little difficult to apply when it comes to buying a take-away shop or restaurant in a busy high street environment. But the Chinese in U.K. still very much believe in the great forces of energy of "wind and water" and so will call in one of the many Fung Shui experts who live here to advise them on how to get the best Fung Shui for their premise.

And so, on the entrances to take-aways, you may see various symbols and characters. In restaurants the cash till will be placed in a specific location. Also when you sit at your table in the restaurant you may not be aware that your table and those around you have been carefully positioned and that the decor,

Master Chu praying in his centre. ▼

Door God on a New Territories house.

Of course there are no such ancestral halls in Britain, but in nearly every Chinese home here, just as in Hong Kong or China, you can see a black and white portrait of a dead ancestor, probably the parents or grandparents. This is to emphasise the fact that, although dead, a senior member of the family is there in spirit.

Traditional religious beliefs and customs are still widely practised by the Chinese in the U.K. They are felt to be important enough for many British Chinese to make trips back to their homeland to attend special festivals, such as Ching Ming (the worshipping of ancestors).

Next time you are in a take-away have a good look around!

including the colour scheme, has been carefully chosen. You may also notice a fish tank of goldfish opposite the restaurant entrance, a very common sight, all to bring good fortune from the Fung Shui.

At home, even the positioning of furniture in the living room and the bedrooms is important to the Chinese. If illness or bad luck befalls a family a Fung Shui expert will be quickly brought in to solve the problem through getting the Fung Shui correct. Outside a Chinese home or shop you may also find an octagonal shaped mirror, which is called a Pa Kwa. This is to ward off bad spirits, and so great care is taken to fix it up at the right place, at the right time and on the right day. You may think that this is superstition and that the Chinese are a superstitious people, but such ideas and customs may be considered as an expression of their religious and spiritual feelings. Other people in the world also have similar beliefs.

Another significant part of Chinese religious life is ancestor worship. It is very much a part of the Confucian tradition, but is also followed by Buddhists and Taoists. In Hong Kong and China, especially in villages where there is a clan lineage, there are ancient temples or halls where the ceremony of praying, offering food and burning incense is performed.

Posters in a Chinatown business.

FESTIVAL

Celebrating
Chinese Festivals

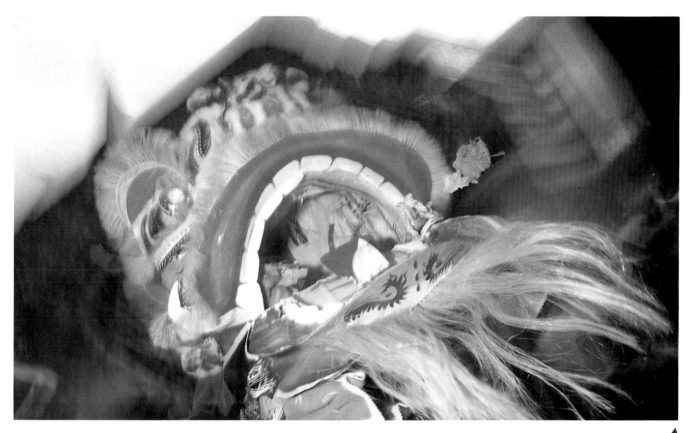

INTRODUCTION

If you have been one of the many thousands of people who every year attend the Chinese New Year Festival in the chinatowns of London or Manchester you will have noticed the colourful dragon and lion dances that snake through the huge crowds of people who are enjoying themselves. All around there is much fun and amusement; the restaurants are full, and many people come out dressed in their best clothes.

The New Year Festival, also known as the Spring Festival, is just one of a number of festivals that the Chinese celebrate throughout their lunar year. It would be very time consuming to count up and list them all. Some festivals are celebrated in one particular area or region by a particular religious group, eg Buddhists or Taoists, and so only involve a limited number of people. There are, however, several other major festivals which occur during the year that are celebrated by all Chinese.

It is necessary to fully understand how important these festivals are to the Chinese people as they are very much connected with the workings of Heaven and Earth and the way in which Nature and the humans exist within this framework. And, as we look more closely at some of the major festivals this importance and the strength of feeling behind it will become obvious. Let us start with the biggest festival, which is the New Year Festival.

NEW YEAR

Chinese New Year is the biggest and most lively of all the Chinese festivals. As it is a lunar festival there is no fixed date and New Year's Day can come any time between late January and the end of February. The main spirit of the festival is "renewal". The old year goes and with it all the old bad luck and problems. New Year is the time to start afresh.

New Year is also a time for family reunion (which is why so many Chinese living in the U.K. go back to Hong Kong or to China. Many people in Hong Kong visit relatives in China). On New Year's Eve the family will gather together at home for a New Year's Eve meal in the evening. No one wants to go to bed early that evening as they want to witness the old year out and the new year in. In fact, on the New Year's Eve, people are not supposed to go to bed at all; it is believed that by not sleeping they help to prolong the life of their parents. This is called "Sau Soy" ("guarding the aged"). Many of

A boy passes under New Year lanterns in Hong Kong.
▶

Flower Market in Hong Kong.
▼

the take-away owners across the U.K., once they have closed their business for the night, will stay up celebrating and visiting friends and relatives or going to a local temple. There are a number of such temples around, and visiting them is very popular. In Hong Kong the families go out to the special flower markets that are packed with people buying their peach blossom trees and fresh flowers. In Britain this, of course, is not possible. Some people get friends or relatives to bring over peach blossom trees from Hong Kong, but otherwise they rely on high street flower shops!

There are a number of things to be done before the New Year's Day arrives. As it is a time for renewal every family is busy spring cleaning the home. After that it is time for stocking up on food and drink for the celebrations. Parents also get ready trays with New Year sweets on and the red packets of lucky money. People also try to settle all their outstanding debts.

Six days before the New Year's Eve, on the 24th day of the twelfth moon the "Kitchen God" or "To Tei Kung" is supposed to leave for heaven. On this day his picture is taken down for renewal. It is ceremonially burned to send him on his way after he is worshipped with incense and candles and given a meal of sticky, sweet things.

At New Year the house is decorated with red, lucky papers, stuck on each side of and above the door. Other papers are stuck up in different parts of the house. These papers have Chinese characters on them, referring to wealth, longevity and the gift of sons. Also stuck up at the same time are pictures of the

"Door Gods". They are to protect against the most evil of spirits.

In Hong Kong the New Year would be the start of several days' holiday, like Christmas time in Britain. That is not possible for the Chinese here, and so they may close their take-away or restaurant for the New Year's Day only.

A boy in Hong Kong passes a couplet that says 'Kung Hei Fat Choy'.
▼

The New Year festival lasts for 15 days. Here is a brief summary of what happens on each day:

Day 1 (New Year's Day)

It is the custom for all members of the family to wear new clothes. In Britain the Chinese will close their businesses for the day and visit friends and relatives. They would also perhaps watch some Chinese videos.

Day 2 This is "Kai Nien" or the beginning of the year. People again visit each other and exchange gifts and lucky money.

Day 3 In Hong Kong people go to temples to hope for good fortune. It is also commonly known as "Squabble Day", and so people refrain from calling on families and acquaintances.

Day 4 The day of welcoming back the "Kitchen God" after his visit to Heaven.

Day 5 Known as the "Day of the God of Wealth". Most businesses re-open on this day.

Day 6 You can again start to tidy your house.

Day 7 This day is everyone's birthday ("Yan Yat").

Day 8 Traditional Chinese families will worship all the gods in Heaven.

Day 9 Jade Emperor's birthday. He is the most superior of gods worshipped by the Taoists. Incense is the main offering.

Day 10-14

In the villages of the New Territories any local family to whom a son has been born during the past year is supposed to bring a lantern to the village ancestral hall and light the good luck lanterns to bring good health to their son.

Day 15

The lantern festival which marks the end of the New Year period. In Hong Kong it is an occasion for public lantern displays, processions and dragon dances.

▲ *Dressing a plum tree bought on New Year's Eve from the flower market. Note the Kum quat tree in foreground, also for good fortune.*

Lantern festival in Hong Kong to mark the ▲
end of the New Year period.

In Britain the New Year is a time for the Chinese to put on a huge celebration that all people can share in in chinatowns like London, Manchester and Liverpool. Thousands of people gather to visit the restaurants and watch the various events. Manchester is considered a Dragon City, which means that it has a dragon that dances through the streets from the Town Hall to the chinatown. At 200 feet long it is one of the longest Chinese dragons in the Western world.

The Chinese New Year celebrations in the U.K. chinatowns normally take place on the first Sunday after New Year, so look out for them!

◀ *Fireworks at New Year in Hong Kong harbour.*

▶
The lion dancing in the streets around Manchester Chinatown.

▲
**The dragon passes
Manchester Town
Hall during New
Year celebrations.
It is one of the
longest dragons
outside of China.**

▲
Firecrackers, Chinatown.

◄
**The firecrackers are
very, very loud.**

CHING MING FESTIVAL

After the New Year the next major festival in the Chinese calendar is that of Ching Ming. It stems from celebrating the departure of cold, wintry days. Ching Ming, also sometimes known as "The Pure Brightness Festival", has many ancient ceremonies taking place during the day, with the most important and widely performed one being that of cleaning and sweeping the graves of ancestors. Like the ancient Egyptians many Chinese believe that the souls of the dead ancestors need looking after, and offerings of food, drinks and incense are brought to the graves. Paper money is sometimes burned at the graves, in order that steady income would reach the departed ancestors.

It is no different for the Chinese in Britain who will make a special effort to go to the local cemetery at Ching Ming. Often, the Chinese in Britain will organise a visit to Hong Kong that coincides with Ching Ming, so that they can visit the graves of their ancestors there too. This visit may also extend to China if, as is common, there are ancestors buried there.

THE DRAGON BOAT FESTIVAL

The Dragon Boat Festival is one of the most exciting of the festivals to watch, especially if you are lucky enough to be able to see the event in Victoria Harbour in Hong Kong. Teeth are bared and muscles bulge as the teams plunge their oars in and out of the water in time to the beat of the drum at the far end of the decorous long boat as they compete to win the races. In Hong Kong harbour the event now attracts teams from all over the world. This international interest has led to increasing numbers of events being staged in Britain with several mostly non-Chinese teams competing.

So why dragon boats? In many cultures the dragon is a feared monster, but in China, however, people have always looked upon the dragon as a kindly river

► *The Dragon Boat day is a day for the family to enjoy a day out together. This event is in Tai Po in the New Territories away from the razzmatazz of the event in Victoria Harbour.*

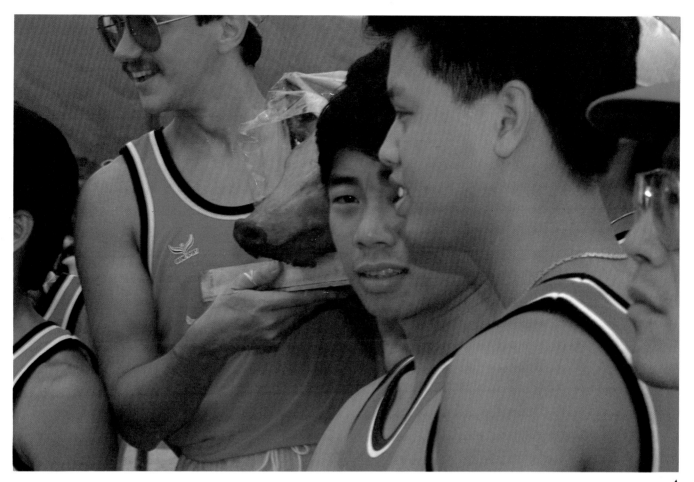

▲
A victorious Dragon Boat team with their prize of a roast pig.

deity who means to help them. The Dragon Boat Festival is mostly associated with the story of Qu Yuan who was a famous politician in the state of Chu in ancient China. Qu Yuan tried to help the King of Chu against the more powerful state of Qin, but his enemies split him from his King. He was exiled, and while he was wandering he wrote many beautiful poems. Later on, when his native Chu had been defeated by Qin he committed suicide by drowning. People began to mourn him and remember him as a wise man. They had tried to find his body in the river, and even today the dragon boats are meant to be looking for his body.

One of the popular foods eaten on the day of the Dragon Boat Festival is a lotus leaf-wrapped ball of glutinous rice with various kinds of fillings such as green beans, peanuts and dates. It is called "Zong Zi". It is the eating of the "Zong Zi" which is the only way most of the Chinese in Britain mark the Dragon Boat Festival.

On the festival day it is a good omen if it rains, so that should be no problem in an English summer!

THE MID AUTUMN FESTIVAL

The seventh, eighth and the ninth months of the Chinese lunar calendar are the months of autumn. The autumn is a period of great happiness, because that is the season traditionally when the harvest is collected from the farms. The bigger the harvest, the less chance of shortages or starvation in the bleak winter months.

On the fifteenth day of the eighth lunar month, which is exactly the middle of the autumn season, the moon is at its greatest distance from the earth and is, according to the Chinese way of putting it, "perfectly round". This day is celebrated in China as the Mid-Autumn Festival.

There are many legends and stories about the moon and the mid-autumn festival, but one particular custom continues until the present day. On the day of the festival all Chinese people exchange gifts and presents and, among the many delicacies cooked, the moon cakes are the most important. In the past the moon cakes were shaped in the form of animals (particularly rabbit, because there are many stories about the rabbit and the moon), flowers or goddesses. The cakes were filled with sugar paste, almonds, oranges, melons and even bits of beef and ham. Today, amongst the Chinese communities all over the world, moon cakes are eaten on the day of the Mid-Autumn Festival.

One interesting fact about moon cakes is how they were used in the past to pass on secret messages. During the time of the Mongol invasion, when the Chinese nation went through much suffering and cruelty, there were many rebellions against the invaders. On one occasion secret orders to kill the Mongols were written on small slips of papers that were hidden in the moon cakes sold in a particular town.

It is always possible to guess the approach of the Mid-Autumn festival in Britain by paying a visit to the Chinese supermarkets where shelves will suddenly be packed with bright metal yellow and red tins of moon cakes imported from Hong Kong. For some people their tins of moon cakes are brought by relations from Hong Kong.

In the larger British chinatowns special events are now organised where moon cakes are handed out to all, and there might be a spectacular firework display too. The children will also carry delicately coloured paper lanterns lit-up by a candle on the inside. In Hong Kong this event is a wonderful time for children.

▶ *Children in Chinatown at Mid-Autumn, enchanted by the beautiful lanterns.*

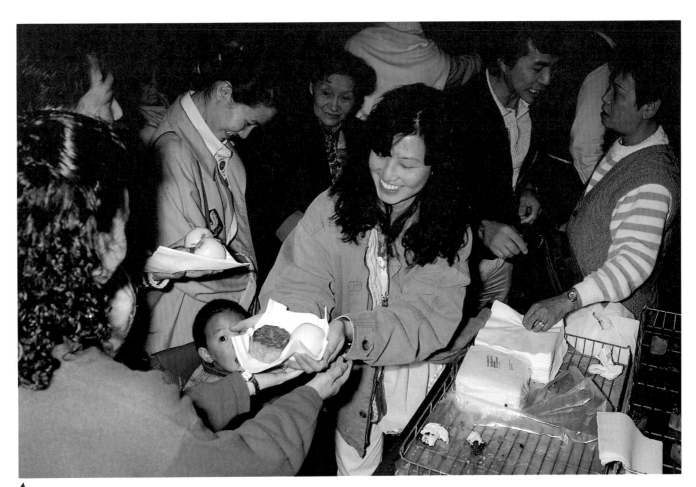

▲
Handing out mooncakes and apples at a Mid-Autumn event in Manchester Chinatown.

Children enjoying the Mid-Autumn festival in Chinatown.
▼

LANGUAGE

Chapter Ten

The Chinese Language
- Spoken and Written

▲
**Artist Edward Ho with
poems that he has written
on his living room wall.**

What do we mean when we ask "Do you speak Chinese?" to a Chinese person? When we think of Europe we take it for granted that there are many different peoples, and so it should be no surprise that a country as large as China has 56 ethnic groups. Most of these ethnic groups, just as in Europe, have their own language or dialect. The largest ethnic group is the Han.

In 1949 when the Communists came to power and founded the People's Republic of China they wanted to ensure that all the people of China had a common language, a national language. The dialect chosen was Mandarin (Putonghua), a very well known dialect originally spoken in the northern part of China.

Although Mandarin is now spoken by the people all over China the various regional dialects are still maintained. Shanghainese (from the Shanghai region in the east of China), Fukinese (from the Fujian province in the south east) and Cantonese (from the large southern province of Canton, now called Guangdong) are amongst the most widely spoken of these dialects.

Despite the fact that many of these dialects share similar characteristics it would be true to say that a Mandarin only speaker and a Hong Kong Cantonese only speaker, for instance, would not be able to understand each other in conversation.

The people of Hong Kong, which is located on the southern tip of Canton province, are mainly Cantonese in origin; and so Cantonese has become the principal language spoken in Hong Kong. Most

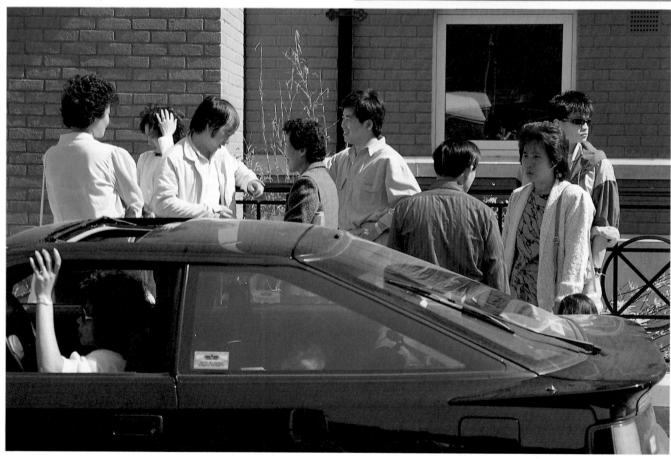

▲ **Conversations across the Chinese world.**
◄
◄

of the Chinese living in Britain are from Hong Kong and therefore Cantonese is the language most commonly heard in Britain. Many of the Chinese living here, however, are Hakka people, the earliest settlers in Hong Kong, and so they speak Hakkanese dialect too.

The Chinese language is very different to the English language. There are no less than 450,000 words and idiomatic phrases in the "classical" language

(in English we might call the language of Shakespeare our "classical" language), although a vocabulary of about 3500 words would be enough to get by in everyday conversation.

Spoken Chinese relies on the way a word is pronounced for meaning - to find out which "tone" is used. Many words have several different meanings depending on the tone used: eg "ma", meaning horse, spoken as "maa" (with a level sound) as against "ma", meaning mother, spoken as "mah" (an upward sound). So please make sure that you get your tone correct when talking to your mother!

For example, in Cantonese...   *and in Mandarin...*

"s͡iu" means laugh or smile, *while...*   "s͜iu" also means small or little;

"d͡a" means big or large, *while...*   "d͜a" also means hit;

The grammar, too, is different in Chinese. Chinese do not conjugate the verb, so there is no past, present or future tense; the verb always stays in the infinitive. To show whether the conversation is in the past, present or future tenses the Chinese have to qualify the verb. For example,

Yesterday   )
Now   ) we go to town.
Tomorrow   )

There is also no "he" or "she" or plural. For example, "I saw a greengrocer and he was eating plums" would have to be, in Chinese, "Earlier on I see a male greengrocer eat some plum".

Here are some simple Cantonese words and phrases to learn:

One = "Yat" (cut the sound off)

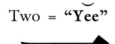

Two = "Yee"

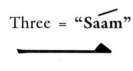

Three = "Saam"

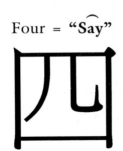

Four = "Say"

四

Five = "Mm"

五

Six = "Luk" (cut the sound off)

六

Seven = "Tchat"

七

Eight = "Bah" (Ba as in Bat)

八

Nine = "Gow"

九

Ten = "Sap"

十

Yes = "H͡ai"

係

No = "M̄mh͡ai"

唔係

Thank You = "D̆odtzer"

多謝

My name is John
="N̄g͡awge m̄eng ğil j͡o"

I am ten years old
="N̄gaw ğum l̄in s̄ap s͡oy"

I can speak Chinese
="N̄gaw s͡ic ḡong j̆ungman"

I can speak English
="N̄gaw s͡ic ḡong y̆ingman"

The common form of greeting for the Chinese is not "How are you?" but "Have you eaten yet?". This is how you say it (in Cantonese): "N͡ay s̆ic j͡aw f͡an m̆ei?"

WRITTEN CHINESE

Written Chinese is the great unifier of the Chinese language and the Chinese people. Whether one speaks Mandarin, Cantonese or whatever, the written language is the same.

Written Chinese does not consist of words but what are called characters which, thousands of years ago, were originally pictograms. As the written language is based on these "characters" and not having a phonetic alphabet, it is possible to be able to speak Chinese and not be able to read it, and vice versa.

There are at least 56,000 characters in existence, although fewer than 10,000 are still in use. A desk dictionary lists some 8,500 items, and a Chinese intellectual may use between 6,000 and 7,000. A learner of the language needs to know a minimum of 1,200 to 1,500 characters in order to read non-classical texts.

Each character consists of a series of strokes which must be memorised. This requires a considerable feat of human memory and explains why so many of the Chinese children living in Britain, who have a more limited need of written Chinese than their counterparts in Hong Kong or China, have to attend Chinese Sunday School to study written Chinese.

Words do not always coincide with characters, for over 50% of the 'words' in modern, standard Chinese consist of two or more characters. For example,

WOMEN	+	HORSE	=	MOTHER

女　　馬　　媽

There are two written forms of Chinese. The "traditional" characters (numerous and complex) are used in Hong Kong, Taiwan, Singapore and around the world. The "simplified" characters, sometimes called Pinyin, are used in China, where they were introduced as part of the reforming of the Chinese language undertaken by the Chinese government in 1954. The difference between the two may be illustrated as follows:

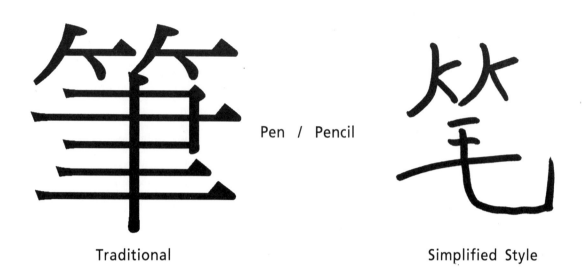

Pen / Pencil

Traditional   Simplified Style

Follow the steps and learn how to write the Characters below:

Man = **Yan**   Big = **Dai**

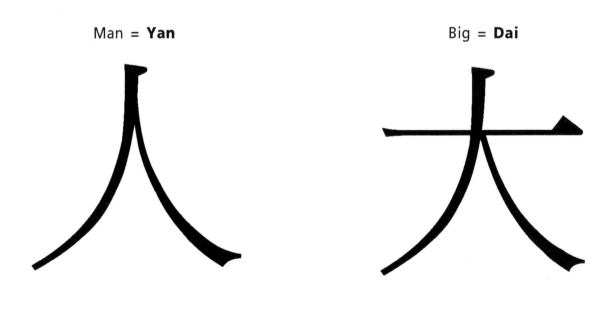

Middle = **Jung**

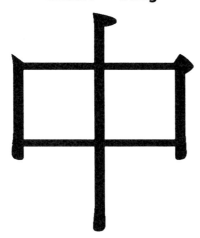

Cooked Rice = **Fan**

Kingdom = **Guo**

Uncooked Rice = **Mai**

City = **Sing**

CUISINE

Chapter Eleven

The Riches of Chinese Cuisine

▲
Dim Sum baskets steaming in a busy restaurant kitchen.

Chinese cuisine is one of the richest and most varied cuisines in the world. It is also, by far, the most familiar element of Chinese culture for people all over the U.K., through frequent visits to the numerous Chinese restaurants and take-aways in our towns and cities.

As we tuck in to our succulent spare ribs and other delicious dishes in a Chinese restaurant (or even at home, now) it is worth reflecting on the fact that Chinese cuisine is a cuisine that has been developed over thousands of years by the vast population of China (much of it impoverished) to guard against the ever present threat of famine. Much of China's culinary heritage has been created by a people who have developed an acute sense of famine foods to help them to survive in hard times.

ROOTS OF CHINESE CUISINE

Despite the fact that China has only 7% of the earth's cultivated land (which is about one eighth of China's land area) the country has to feed 22% of the world's population. Today there are nearly 1.2 billion Chinese mouths to feed. The Chinese have, therefore, had to explore and discover the nutritional value of a great many plants, roots, vegetables, animals and fish. If it can at all be

helped, no part of the food is wasted in case any of the nutritional value it may possess is lost. The skill of the Chinese people, then, has been to create a cuisine which makes such ingredients as chicken claws and fish lips not only edible but tasty.

To cope with the huge dietary needs of the population the Chinese have to farm their lands very efficiently. Nearly 80% of the land is given to growing grains, of which the two most important are rice and

wheat. Forming the staple diet of the Chinese, rice is principally grown in the warmer southern half of China, where rainfall is more predictable and the soil retains water well, whilst wheat is grown in the colder regions of the north.

Other important crops are sweet potatoes, maize, peanuts and chillies. Nearly 120 different types of vegetables are grown, most in the warmer southern regions. It is in the north, however, that a key

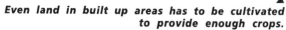

Varieties of pulses on sale in a market in China.
▼

▲
Even land in built up areas has to be cultivated to provide enough crops.

▲
A young boy loads the husks of rice into sacks during rice harvest, Shanghai, China.

Salted fish hanging up in the sun in Hong Kong.
▼

vegetable in Chinese dishes, the soya bean, was developed. Now grown all over China, many food products have been developed from the soya bean (which is very high in protein) such as the famous "soy sauce" used for flavouring and bean curd, "to-fu", which is sometimes called "meat without bones".

Meat eating is very popular, with pork, beef and chicken the most commonly eaten meats. Nearly 800 types of fish are farmed from the great rivers of China, the Pacific Ocean and the China Sea. Prawns, oysters and lobsters are all great delicacies, and shark's meat is much valued for soups and other dishes.

In order to store food and, for obvious practical reasons, make it last as long as possible, the Chinese have developed many preserved foods, such as pickled cabbage and turnip, dried or salted fish, oyster sauce, cured ducks and sausages and the intriguingly named Hundred Year Old Egg (a duck egg cocooned in clay or soil and left).

CHINESE FOOD IN BRITAIN

Regular exposure to Chinese cuisine at restaurants and take-aways has introduced the non-Chinese in the U.K. to many of the exotic and exciting ingredients in Chinese cooking. This has influenced shopping habits as people decided that they wanted to re-create some of the dishes in their own homes. The demand for Chinese foodstuffs from both Chinese and non-Chinese has led to foods such as ginger, beancurd, beansprouts, Chinese leaves and soy sauce becoming readily available in shops and markets throughout the U.K. It has also meant that meats such as spare ribs, for instance, have become expensive whereas in the past they were thrown away or sold very cheaply.

The Chinese supermarkets that have opened in large cities like London, Manchester, Liverpool and Birmingham to service the needs of the Chinese catering trade now provide all the ingredients that a Chinese person would seek to buy in Hong Kong. These supermarkets are also popular with the non-Chinese; and so it continues, until many aspects of Chinese cuisine — and, therefore the culture — have been absorbed into the everyday life of the U.K.

Many Chinese seek out the open markets to buy fresh fruits, vegetables and fish. In Hong Kong each neighbourhood has its own open air market selling fresh produce, and the people are able to buy whatever is needed for that evening's meal just before it is needed. In the U.K. this is not possible, and so they may visit a market only once or twice a week.

It can be an interesting sight to watch some of the Chinese shopping at a market as they go through various procedures to check the quality of the food, such as tapping the base of a water melon or lifting the gills of a fish. Of course, the other big difference between shopping in the U.K. and shopping in Hong Kong is that there is no haggling over the price here.

UTENSILS

It is a testament to Chinese ingenuity when it comes to the utensils needed in the cooking of Chinese food. If pushed, most Chinese meals could be prepared with just three utensils, ie a wok, chop sticks (which are used for eating too) and a cleaver.

The wok and chop sticks are great inventions. The wok is a simple, durable and extremely versatile round-bottomed iron pan which can be used for stir-frying (a speedy form of frying, using not too much oil), steaming, boiling, poaching and even baking and roasting. The Chinese like to fry their ingredients, especially vegetables, very quickly over a high heat in order to seal in all the nutrients. A take-away will have between two and four large woks in use.

The wide bladed cleaver is used primarily for cutting meat and vegetables. The flat of the blade can pound and crush garlic and ginger as well as scoop ingredients off the chopping board.

Other utensils and equipment that you might find in a Chinese kitchen are perforated spoons, wire mesh ladles and earthenware cooking pots which are good for slow cooking. Arguably the most important aid to Chinese cooking invented in modern

Mr. Kwok stirfrying beansprouts in a wok.
▶

Marie Loong serves the rice out of the family rice cooker.

Mr. Wong grows a variety of Chinese vegetables in his Liverpool garden.
▼

times is the electric rice cooker which automatically cooks and steams rice.

Like Chinese foodstuffs, all the utensils are available in Chinese supermarkets and also, increasingly, in general department stores and shops throughout the U.K.

EATING AT HOME

Most people's experience of Chinese cuisine remains that of restaurants or take-aways, with sweet and sour pork being the most popular dish. This, however, would rarely be eaten at the home of a Chinese family.

Many of the Chinese in the U.K. have, through necessity, to eat their meals during the opening times of their business. Meal times are an important time when the family can gather together; and so the food is especially cooked. The family members stick to traditional Chinese cuisine, which is not the same as that served to the customers. A typical meal will contain a soup course (consisting of a watery soup made from perhaps lotus seeds, vegetables and pulses) followed by rice, which is the "fan", and meat and vegetable dishes, the "cai". Whereas most of the customers will order fried rice, the Chinese family will always eat boiled rice.

Each person will have their own bowl of rice, but the family or the group share several different "cai" dishes placed in the centre of the table. Dishes such as salted fish and preserved vegetables steamed in mince, stir fried meat, Chinese vegetables and steamed chicken are all very popular with Chinese families.

Before the meal starts respect will be paid to the elders around the table (normally children to their parents by asking them to "eat rice" (fan).) It is considered rude to pile up meats or vegetables on the rice. The best way to eat rice is to put the bowl to your mouth and scoop it in with your chopsticks.

EATING OUT

The Chinese love to eat out. That is why on Sundays, when their businesses are closed, they pour into the chinatowns to visit the restaurants. They like to take their guests out, and eating out is an important social element in the culture. Business is often conducted around a restaurant table rather than in the confines of an office.

Going to a restaurant is often called "Yam Char" or, literally, drinking tea. In Hong Kong the restaurants are packed from 6.00 am until 2.00 pm, and many people go to "Yam Char" each day. Tea is served with delicious snacks called "dimsums" which arrive in steaming hot, bamboo baskets. Some of the most popular dimsums are "Siu Mai" (a parcel of steamed pork, prawns, mushrooms and vegetables), "Cheung Fan" (rice roll with either a beef, barbecued pork or prawn filling), steamed chicken claw and "har gau" (a steamed prawn dumpling).

REGIONAL STYLES AND SCHOOLS OF COOKING

There are four main regional varieties of Chinese cooking.

1) Cantonese style:

This is a very popular style of cooking from the south of China. Most of the Chinese restaurants in Britain, run by the Hakkanese people, serve Cantonese food. Steamed foods, particularly dimsums, are an important part of Cantonese food. Rice is the staple "fan", because most rice in China grows in the south. As the south is fertile with plenty of rainfall and mild winters there is plenty of choice in fruits, vegetables, meats and fishes.

2) Northern style:

This comes from the northern part of China where Beijing, the capital, is located. Rice does not grow here because of the cold, harsh climate. This is the land of wheat farming or millet and barley farming. From the flour of these cereals noodles, steamed breads and buns, pancakes and dumplings are made. Mutton and duck are more popular than pork, and there are many flavourings and seasonings used, such as vinegar, garlic, coriander, onions and leeks. The famous dish of Peking Duck belongs to the northern style of cooking.

3) Shanghai style:

In the east of China lies the great port of Shanghai. It is built at the point where the River Yangtse meets the ocean. In this fertile eastern region there is plenty of fresh food available, and the long coastline provides a ready supply of fish. The common methods of cooking are stir-frying, steaming and stewing. Shanghai has long been a cosmopolitan port, and so the Shanghai style of cooking takes into consideration foreigners' tastes.

4) Sichuan style:

Far away, in the west of China, lies the remote Sichuan province, a mountainous and rugged land. The river Yangtse flows through

◄
A young girl during the family visit to a restaurant for Yam Char.

▲
Mr. & Mrs. Cheung enjoy preparing Chinese food at home when they have the time.

the area, and there is an abundance of food. Here the local people have developed unique dishes, full of taste and nutrition; but the food is hot and spicy, because in this part of China there are many other Asian influences. Chillies are used in great quantity in the preparation of the dishes.

(Consult Appendix 5 for some simple Chinese delicacies and an illustration showing how to use chopsticks).

A rice shop in Hong Kong selling varieties of rice.
▼

ARTS

Chapter Twelve

Chinese Arts

▲
*Mr. La, a local artist making
a sign for a take-away.*

The video goes on, and suddenly the hi-tech TV is filled with pictures from a Hong Kong costume drama that depicts political intrigue and romance from the Sung, Tang or Ching Dynasty.

The actors are costumed perfectly to match the era whilst the sets are lavishly decorated to set the style for that dynasty. The programme producers have no problem in making sure that all the effects and artifacts are accurate. Whether what they are depicting took place a hundred or a thousand years before, they will be familiar with the beautiful paintings from ancient times that document the architecture, fashions and art from dynasties deep in history.

As the accompanying music, based on Chinese classical themes, booms from the stereo speakers linked to the TV, fruit is offered around the room from a reproduction Ming Dynasty bowl. On the mantlepiece are reproduction vases, bought from an English wholesaler, filled with silk flowers. Next to them are miniature urns decorated in brocade.

Above the mantlepiece is a large rosewood charm suspended between two bright red knotted string patterns. On the opposite wall is a wooden panelled picture that features figures in a landscape from the Tang Dynasty, made from carved, polished and coloured shells.

Phoenix Head
▼

Mrs. Loong with paintings on the wall of her shop. ▲

Meanwhile, at the far end of the lounge, a computer scans and prints out a traditional motif for use on a restaurant menu. Calendars featuring beautiful

examples of Chinese painting hang around the house. Those from previous years considered of particular beauty are rolled up and kept.

This Chinese art around the house or the work place, which can also be seen in Hong Kong or wherever the Chinese have settled, serves as a reminder of how important Chinese culture is to the everyday lives of the Chinese in Britain. As well as being beautiful, the decorative reminders of their ancestral heritage, the paintings, calligraphy and other artifacts are full of symbolic meaning which the Chinese take very seriously. For instance, in Chinese restaurants, you may well be able to see a dragon or a phoenix arranged around a Chinese character, in bright red, which says "Double Happiness". This character will be strategically placed so that the bride and the groom can sit beneath it during the wedding banquet, with the dragon and the phoenix hovering magnificently overhead. It is believed this will bring good fortune. It is a good example of how something is both beautiful and decorative but also has a meaning and purpose.

TWO MAJOR PHASES OF CHINESE ART

The history of Chinese Art may be divided into two phases. In the first phase, during the Stone and Bronze ages, the art is influenced greatly by the idea that natural objects such as rocks, trees and animals were supposed to possess souls and, in particular, the souls of the dead ancestors. This idea is called "animism". It was to please the soul(s) of the dead that art was used for depicting natural objects.

The second phase is the period of the great historical dynasties of China, based on religions such as Buddhism and Taoism. This second phase gives us much of the wonderful art that has now become familiar in the West. The art of this phase is full of complex religious symbols. Chinese "classic" art reached its peak during the Sung Dynasty (AD 960-1279), notably in paintings and ceramics that mostly depicted natural creations such as birds, fish, flowers, plants and mountains.

CHINESE LOVE OF NATURE

From the arts of painting, poetry, writing and music it is obvious that the Chinese have a deep love of nature. There have been times during Chinese history, such as the Sung Dynasty, when certain flowers, fruits and plants have assumed great symbolic significance. Pine, for example, inspired thoughts of longevity, bamboo the suppleness needed to bend with life's troubles, and the mulberry filial piety.

Seasons were also depicted. The peony tree indicated the delights of spring and its flowers of riches and honour. The lotus is regarded as a symbol for a friendly summer full of spiritual purity, creative power and the blessing of immortal gods. The chrysanthemum shared the charm of autumn, whilst the wild plum was for severe winter. At New Year households still display a peach blossom tree in order to bring prosperity during the following year. In Britain this is not really possible as it is difficult and expensive to get hold of. Therefore only a few restaurants will display it, with households making do with flowers such as chrysanthemum and peony instead.

▲
Chinese lions used to bring fortune and protection.

MEANING AND MYSTERY IN CHINESE ART

Chinese art inspires curiosity, making you want to explore and understand more. There is an air of mystery attached to it. Often looking at Chinese painting is like looking at a scene from a fairy tale. "A Chinese picture", as the saying goes, "is a voiceless poem". A country landscape is held by the Chinese artist to correspond to phases of the human soul; water is regarded as the blood of the mountains; grass and trees are like life, while mist and cloud are the complexion. Mountains are considered to be the face, whilst houses and fences are like the eyebrows and eyes. The retired scholar represents the spirit of the countryside.

Chinese paintings were done on scrolls, often silk, and were to be unrolled to view. This made the approach of the Chinese artist different to that of a western one. Chinese artists indicated "space" by choice of colour, the blurring of outlines and the use of overlapping images of different heights. Often paintings depict a minute human being travelling through a landscape of soaring mountains and waterfalls. This was meant to signify how insignificant man was as opposed to the force and endurance of nature!

Chinese painting is characterised by delicate brush strokes based on calligraphy. The art of calligraphy is held in very high regard by the Chinese. An individual is judged not just by the content of what he or she has written but also by the quality of the brush and ink calligraphy that give form to the

content. There are several distinctive styles of calligraphy, and it is said that the choice of style is as much a moral decision as an aesthetic one. "The way a master calligrapher wielded his brush was a window onto his soul", it was said. In a temple, by displaying "silence" in the form of calligraphy, one is supposed to be helped to purify one's thoughts.

CHINESE ART IN BRITAIN

Calligraphy and other art forms, particularly painting, have provided a way of making a living for many Chinese in Britain. There are several art and craft shops in the larger chinatowns selling all manner of goods ranging from spectacularly beautiful paintings and woodcarvings down to the plastic lucky charms. They also sell greeting cards featuring Chinese designs. Since the 18th century, there has ben a great interest in the West in Chinese art, and so trade is brisk in the shops selling to interested visitors to chinatown.

Chinese artists are also able to make a living. Those who provide their calligraphic skills for restaurant and take-away signs are much in demand. Others, particularly the young artists, have formed arts companies that promote Chinese arts, both modern and traditional, through all forms, such as painting, dance and music.

CHINESE MUSIC

Chinese music is, like Chinese painting, full of symbolic meanings. The earliest Chinese scale of notation consisted of five sounds which were contrasted with five plants, five points, five colours and five elements. These represented the Emperor, ministers, people, affairs of state and material objects respectively. This is why we associate particular types of melody and chord sequences with Chinese "style" music.

As with all Chinese art forms, many of the traditional aspects of Chinese music are still very much a part of modern times. This can be seen most

◄
Artist Edmund Ho doing calligraphy.

clearly in Chinese pop music. Cantonese pop music, known as Canto-Pop, is the most popular form of music listened to by the Chinese today. Spreading from Hong Kong, its stars can be seen on posters in the homes and shops of the Chinese from Toronto to Beijing and from Sydney to London. Even though it is set in the modern age and is heavily influenced by western pop music (sentimental love songs and "cover" versions of western pop songs being very popular), Canto-Pop is filled with melodies and musical quotes from traditional Chinese folk and classical music. Indeed, many Canto-Pop stars make modern versions of traditional songs.

Again we can see how the culture and traditions are maintained in a modern setting. Many Chinese teenagers are very aware of traditional Chinese melodies. We in the West, on the whole, have a much more limited knowledge of our traditional music.

Many of the Canto-Pop stars can also perform songs from the Chinese opera. Chinese opera is very different to Western opera both in musical content and presentation. The popular operas are often stories set during the old dynasties. Many of them, with regional variations, can often be seen being performed in the streets of China and Hong Kong to an appreciative local audience. All the characters wear make-up that instantly reveals who they are and whether they are good or evil characters. Their movements are heavily stylised to indicate things such as fighting or that they are getting on a horse.

During the opera performance much of the audience will continue to talk. This is not through rudeness, but that they are discussing the story and performance. The audience will often applaud if a performer sings a particularly striking note!

FASHION AND JEWELLERY

Today's fashions are different to those we associate with ancient China. For example, the emperor's dress in those times was unique, and designed according to strict rules laid down by the "Board of Ceremonies" which was like a Ministry of Fashion. The emperor was the only person in China who was allowed to have his clothes embroidered with dragons on his gold robes. On all official garments and robes

Musicians in Xian, China.
▼

there were various insignia embroidered with symbolic images of the sun, moon, stars, mountains, flames of fire, rice etc.

Working in a take-away shop is hot, with plenty of grease and fat from cooking the fish and chips and frying the assorted Chinese meals, and so little thought can be given to fashion. Practical overalls or a chef's jacket are the order of the day. Generally, however, the Chinese attitudes to fashion are simple and conservative.

Traditionally the Hakkanese people wear dark colours and, although the traditional Hakka clothes are not too often seen in Britain, the women will often wear a plain silk jacket with a mandarin collar (called Daikum), a pair of dark slacks, whilst the men may wear something similar. Cantonese people may also traditionally wear similar styles. However it is very common for Hakka and Cantonese to dress in Western style suits and dresses and particularly so for special occassions. Many of the older women pull their hair back from their foreheads, brush it behind the ears and clip it at the back of the head.

Of course attitudes are different amongst the younger generation. They will dress in the latest designer wear either mimicking clothes and hairstyles seen in the Hong Kong magazines or choosing the current fashions in the UK. The hairdressing salons in the Chinatowns are all able to offer the latest Hong Kong hair fashions, and many Chinese brides

▲
A couple dress up in the style of Sung Dynasty for a picture in China.

will go to such a salon to get their hair done before the wedding.

One very famous fashion that we in the West associate with the Chinese, that of the braided queue (like a pony tail), only came into being because of the Manchu tradition of Qing Dynasty. The Manchu rulers forced all to wear this queue as a sign of allegiance to the Emperor, and the custom only died out after the dynasty collapsed.

We must also mention silk, which is gathered from silk worms. From early times China has been famous for its silk, and elegant dresses and blouses made from silk have been worn by Chinese women for centuries and which can be used throughout the four seasons. A traditional long and slim fitting silk dress with a mandarin collar, called the "Cheong Sam", was very popular at the beginning of the 20th century. Nowadays it is worn in Britain by waitresses or ladies at the reception desk at restaurants.

The one thing that the Chinese do enjoy wearing is jewellery. Traditionally they have thought of

▲
*A bride proudly shows off her jewellery to
a guest on her wedding day.*

jewellery as an investment and a security against bad times. This is why gold jewellery is very popular. Jewellery is also worn for protection. Children will wear a silk necklace and a locket to symbolically "fasten" them to life. Gold necklaces and bracelets are popular, while men like to wear gold chains around their necks and wrists, often with a charm attached for good fortune.

Hong Kong has some spectacular jewellery shops displaying a brilliant array of gold items that are sold by weight according to the current price of gold on the Hong Kong stock market. But as Hong Kong is a long way away and since gold is so popular Hong Kong style shops (on a smaller scale) have opened up in British Chinatowns.

Another very popular item of jewellery is jade. It

is believed to offer great protection and help one's health. Very often, if a Chinese person is wearing a jade bracelet (and a great many do) and the bracelet is lost or suddenly breaks without an apparent reason, the person would say that something bad has or is about to happen, but would take comfort from the fact that the jade would have cushioned the blow from this bad thing. Jade is therefore regarded with reverence, and one can often see Chinese asking about and discussing the qualities of a piece that a friend or relative is wearing.

Jewellery is still very important for the Chinese in Britain, for both young and old. Jade and gold are still worn and, indeed, discussed! Wedding banquets are places to see a bride covered in gold rings and necklaces, bought for her to bring fortune.

◄
*The window of a Hong Kong
jewellery shop.*

MEDICINE

Chapter Thirteen

Chinese Martial Art and Medicine

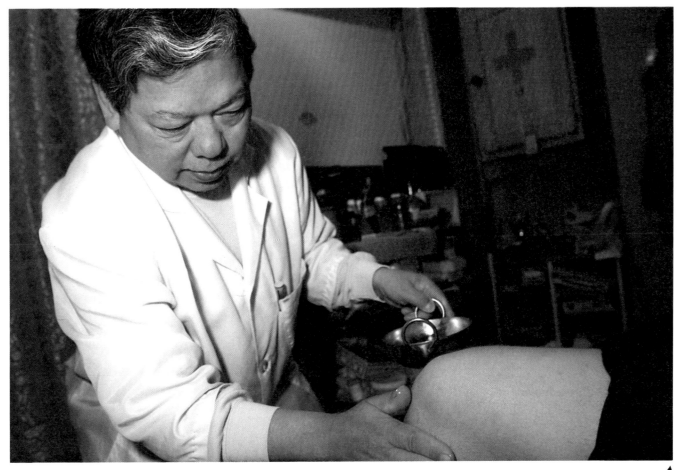

▲
Master Chu treating a patient.

We have read a little about Master Chu in an earlier chapter. Master Chu grew up in a monastery and has studied kung fu all his life. He is now at the stage of learning when he can be called "Master"!

Master Chu works at his martial arts and Chinese medicine centre in the Manchester chinatown. There, for a couple of hours each day between his commitments to his take away shop, and all afternoon on Sundays, he teaches kung fu to his pupils, many of whom are non-Chinese, and practices Chinese medicine on patients (again, many of whom are non-Chinese) who may have travelled from all over Manchester and, quite often, much further afield. Master Chu's small clinic is filled with shelves that are lined with sweet jars jammed full of herbal ingredients. On the walls are medical diagrams of the human body that show the important "acupoints" which are the body's pressure points. In between treating his patients Master Chu keeps an eye on his students who are practising their kung fu in another part of the building.

MARTIAL ART

Martial art, of which kung fu is one of several styles, is a very popular form of exercise. Not only does it build up stamina and physique; it also helps the individual to develop strong self-discipline. Martial art started several centuries ago in monasteries, and it is a method of single combat, to be used in self-defence, not attack. It has a code of ethics which accompanies the physical skills. Virtues such as patience, honour and self-improvement are considered important elements in learning the martial art.

Kung fu originated in China. There are several different styles from different "schools". Master Chu teaches his students a style called "Wing Tsuen". Many of the movements of kung fu are linked to the movements of animals. Often the stance for a particular set of movements mimics the characteristic of an animal. Thus, for instance, in "Wing Tsuen" we have the Ten-Animal form, which is the Dragon form, Snake form, Tiger form, Leopard form, Crane form, Lion form, Elephant form, Horse form, Monkey form and Bear form.

Many Chinese opera artistes learn martial art to enable them to perform the necessary acrobatics on stage. Martial art commands great respect among the Chinese abroad. Some people believe in its supernatural powers. Great exponents such as Bruce Lee and Jackie Chan have become great stars around the world through their kung fu prowess.

Bruce Lee, who died tragically young, is a hero still to many Chinese both in Britain and abroad as well as to many westerners. However, there are less and less Chinese children taking up martial art training in Britain. Not because they dislike it or do not admire it, but because it takes a big commitment and there are many other demands on their time. They must study, help in the business and on Sundays must go to Sunday School to learn Chinese. Master Chu, however, teaches a number of non-Chinese in the skills of martial art; and many of them perform the lion and dragon dances. Master Chu also teaches Chinese medicine to his students, so that they can treat the injuries and illnesses of their fellow artists.

CHINESE MEDICINE

Over the past few years what is termed "alternative medicine" has become more and more popular in the West, including Britain. Chinese medicine is very much included in "alternative medicine". The big difference between Western and Chinese medicine is that the latter places more emphasis on prevention whereas the former is more concerned with cure.

The Chinese also lay great stress on the benefits of natural foods and plants. For example, for over 2000 years, their doctors and physicians have believed that ginger has important healing and anti-inflammatory properties. Scientists in Denmark only "discovered" this in the early 1990s!. Chinese medicine should not be scoffed at!

A doctor in Hong Kong teaches students about acupuncture.
▼

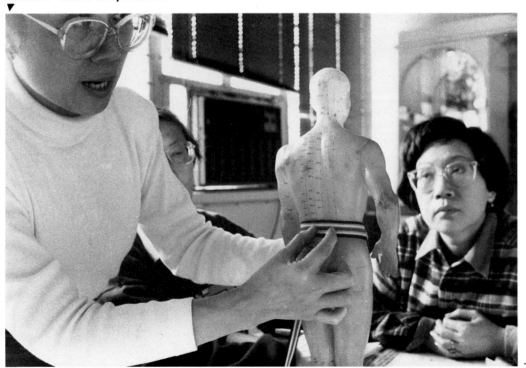

According to Chinese medicine, which is said to have originated with a legendary emperor called Shin Ning who discovered the virtues of various herbs and plants, the human body is made up of five elements. These are fire, water, metals, wood and earth. The body behaves according to the principle of Ying and Yang. Whilst Ying is supposed to be cold and damp, Yang is fiery and windy. Ying and Yang show themselves in signs and symptoms. For example, a dry cough can be considered as Yang, whilst a cough with phlegm would be Yin. Treatment has to be based on the correct composition of the five elements in order to try and restore the harmony of bodily balance. The balance between Ying and Yang must be restored.

Many of the techniques of giving relief to people with muscular or bone injuries or certain allergies are based on the skill of acupuncture. With acupuncture the practitioners of Chinese medicine understand the various energy flows and pressure points of the body to aid recovery. A technique which is finding favour in the West and also based on the principles of acupuncture is reflexology which assumes that the soles of the foot are a map of the body and are massaged to increase blood circulation to various parts of the body.

In order to prevent disease some exercises are recommended; many Chinese people in Britain still perform them daily to bolster their health. One well known exercise is Qi Gong (Chigung) which is a series of breathing exercises said to produce the balance of Yin and Yang. Another is Tai Chi, which was developed from a martial art. Tai Chi is practised every morning by millions of Chinese in China and Hong Kong on the streets and in parks; and we occasionally see a lone Chinese in Britain performing this rather elegant series of slow, fluent movements.

The Chinese in Britain still very much adhere to the principles of Chinese medicine, believing that Ying and Yang govern their bodies. The elderly Chinese, in particular, prefer Chinese medicines and, in order to cater for the demand, the large chinatowns have Chinese herbalist shops, full of exotic items such as ginseng or deer antlers, special Chinese medical practices and acupuncture clinics.

▲ *Tai Chi in a park in China.*

The Chinese in Britain also help each other to provide what they see as essential Chinese medicines! For instance, when a pregnant woman, whose relatives may not be living in Britain, is close to giving birth a lady friend, often older, might well prepare a rather strange "potion" in an earthenware pot. This potion, made of Chinese red vinegar, ginger, pigs' trotters and hard boiled eggs, is prepared some weeks before the birth and has to be eaten once a day, for a month, by the new mother. Also, the mother and the new born baby are not supposed to go out for a month following the birth, but this is not so practical whilst living in Britain. What is important to understand is that the rules and practices associated with Chinese medicine are followed by the vast majority of Chinese people in Britain. Many non-Chinese people are also becoming more aware of the potential benefits of Chinese medicine, and they too are increasingly consulting Chinese doctors and practitioners.

EDUCATION

Chapter Fourteen

Educating Chinese Children in Britain – Tradition and Change

▲
Wai-Hung is the only Chinese boy at his primary school.

Education, and attitudes to it, are closely linked to the culture and traditions of a society. The Chinese have had a deep respect for education ever since their education system began over 2000 years ago during the Han Dynasty (consult the Chronological Table in Appendix 1).

Their desire for their children to succeed in education is today as strong as ever.

Given this fact it is both fascinating and important to consider the traditional attitudes of the Chinese in the U.K. and how they relate to their children's modern day British education. For the education of these children will have an influence on the future of the Chinese and their culture in Britain.

TRADITIONS OF EDUCATION

In order to appreciate the Chinese respect for education it is necessary to look briefly at the history of Chinese education.

First of all, education was not just a matter of gaining knowledge and new skills. It also had to do with one's personality and character. The great philosopher, Confucius, said that a person had to have good manners and etiquette before being able to be called a cultured person. An education was also not complete until the person had learnt to be kind, loyal, respectful and a wise member of his or her family.

It was in China that examinations, as we know them, were developed. Many bright and clever young people had to pass the examination if they wished to serve in the Emperor's Civil Service. Only a few students were selected, and their training was very rigorous. The imperial examination system, which lasted until 1905, was organised at three levels :

district, provincial and metropolitan. Often it would be one man only (for it was always men) from each village who had the opportunity to take the examination, and he would have to pass at all three levels before becoming a Government Officer. These officers or top civil servants came to be known as Mandarins, a description we still use in English to describe a highly placed official.

Becoming a top official obviously brought prestige, status and financial reward to his family and so, not surprisingly, the belief that an education means an opportunity to escape from a life of hardship and drudgery and to be able to "get on" in life has become rooted in the cultural attitudes of the Chinese. Many of the take-away owners in Britain see their life as one of hardship and drudgery. They are therefore very keen to see their children get an education, so that they may have a chance to take up a career in, say, medicine, law, accountancy or computing, jobs which are traditionally seen as being well paid and giving status in society.

A boy studying in a Shanghai Street.
▼

School boys in Hong Kong.

EDUCATION IN BRITAIN

Many Chinese parents living here wonder why there appears to be such a great emphasis on play in the teaching in the U.K. They often regret that there is not enough of rigid studying and learning from books as in Hong Kong. Chinese children are generally expected by their parents to be strong and disciplined and to be able to overcome obstacles and succeed. A strong sense of discipline and work ethic is instilled from an early age, in order that children may learn to cope with the considerable responsibilities that are placed on them while still very young.

Being able to rely on these traditional values has been an important factor in the success of the Chinese children living in the U.K. as they come to terms with the difficulties that their culture duality presents. The academic success of the Chinese children is now increasingly being recognised by the society at large. Research at Manchester University has shown that the British Chinese score very highly in the GCSE and the GCE "A" Level examination, in comparison with other groups of children.

These findings are remarkable if we consider the environment in which this success is achieved. Parents, working late hours in the take-aways or restaurants,

are often unable to participate in their children's education as fully as they might wish or need.

Language is usually the biggest factor here. Not only might the parents' limited knowledge of English lead to misconceptions about the way in which their

Wai-Hung in class.

child is being taught, but it also prevents them getting involved with discussing homework with their children. Attending parents' evenings, which is difficult enough anyway because of working hours, can be a frustrating exercise conversing with the teacher without a translator (rarely available due to the geographic isolation of many Chinese families). Using the child in question as a translator obviously brings problems of its own, and so checking on the child's educational progress is not easy.

▲
Arthur Wong studying for his GCSEs.

Language can lead to additional problems for the child too. There are major differences between English and Cantonese. Chinese children, particularly those who have come from Hong Kong to live here between the ages of seven and fourteen, struggle with English grammar. They have to learn to cope with speaking in one language with their parents and in another at school and with friends.

An uncertain command of English, a fear of losing face and being culturally reserved have sometimes led the Chinese child (often the only one in the school) to stay very quiet in the class. This means that the child can get overlooked by the teacher.

A young boy doing his homework at the back of the take-away.
▼

CULTURAL IDENTITY AND DIVERSITY

As Chinese children, on the one hand, live in a traditional Chinese environment but, on the other hand, are educated in a British one, they will be confronted with many questions about their own cultural identity. Some may struggle to come to terms with their identity; others such as Wai Ling and Wai Hung Cheung, about whom we talked in Chapter 3, are comfortable with being both Chinese and British, seeing it as an advantage.

In many cases the children accept their situation quite readily, and the question of cultural identity becomes important mainly because of its impact on the future of the Chinese culture in the U.K. The Chinese children will become fluent in English through being with English children. They may even speak English at home with their brothers and sisters, leading to an eventual loss of fluency in Cantonese. Subjects as important as history will be taught to them through Western eyes, and the Chinese parents would have to work very hard if they wish to re-enforce the Chinese aspects of their children's lives in order that they maintain the language and the customs.

Ideally the school prepares the children for a life in Britain, whilst the home gives them the sense and security of their Chinese roots and cultural heritage. The Chinese, like other settlers from abroad living in Britain, face the dilemma of how much they can assimilate into British culture and its values while still trying to retain the values and heritage that have been with the Chinese people for nearly 4000 years. They have to find that balance for themselves.

CHINESE SUNDAY SCHOOLS

Language plays an important part in the cultural heritage of any people. The Chinese have tried to ensure that their children maintain the ability to speak Cantonese by setting up Sunday Schools in cities such as London, Manchester, Liverpool and Leeds, where there are large settlements of Chinese. Most of the teachers in these schools are

working in a voluntary capacity. They may be Hong Kong students studying for higher education or the local Chinese who have proficiency in teaching Chinese.

The main purpose of these schools is to teach children to read and write the Chinese language, the language of their parents. Most of the Chinese parents do not speak any English. Since many of them work for long hours it is difficult for them to attend English classes. Children, on the other hand, find it easier to learn Chinese since they would be speaking it at home. They learn English in their normal day school, but by keeping up with their studies in the Sunday School they are able to communicate in Chinese with their parents, other family members and friends.

Some people feel that the Chinese children should not bother to learn their home language but should only learn English as they live in England. They also

Children outside the Chinese Cultural Centre.
▼

argue that it may be confusing for children to learn two languages. That is a wrong attitude to adopt. In fact, more languages one learns, the better. Additionally, many of the children who complete a Sunday school course in Chinese may then be more capable of passing a GCSE in Chinese.

Non-Chinese children also sometimes attend Chinese Sunday schools. They may have Chinese friends, and they may wish to learn more about Chinese culture or just share experiences.

The children who attend the Sunday schools get less time off. They have only one day of rest instead of two. Chinese children, however, look forward to one particular delight, ie. that after school they can drop into a Chinese restaurant for a delicious dimsum meal!

▲
Children at Sunday School.

Boy at Sunday School.
▶

Chapter Fifteen

Conclusion

In this book we have introduced you to the Chinese people of Britain, their history, culture and life style; and we hope that you have enjoyed reading all about the Chinese. In Chapter 1 we gave you the historical background of China and the Chinese people in general. We also looked at the fascinating achievements of the Chinese people over a period of nearly 4000 years. Chapter 2 tells you about Hong Kong's connections with Britain and how the first Chinese settlers arrived in Britain, what occupations they followed and how the Chinatowns developed. In Chapter 3 we have the interesting story of the Cheung Family of Manchester, and we learn about the problems this family has had in settling down in Britain. Chinese life style is discussed in Chapter 4, where we learn about the daily life of a typical Chinese person in Britain. In Chapter 5 we come to know Master Chu, a Kung Fu Master who works in the Chinatown of Manchester. The structure of the Chinese family is described in Chapter 6, while Chapter 7 gives you information on the three most important stages in life : birth, marriage and death, and how the Chinese deal with them. Chapter 8 tells you about the religions of the Chinese and the way they are practised in Britain. The most important Chinese festivals are described in Chapter 9. In Chapter 10 you are introduced to some of the intricacies of the Chinese language. The variety of foods and the cooking styles of the Chinese are explained in Chapter 11, whilst Chapter 12 tells you about the artistic products that the Chinese value and appreciate. Chapter 13 explains you the mysteries of Chinese medicine and martial arts. Chapter 14 looks at some of the problems that the Chinese children face in schools in Britain.

We hope that after reading this book you have come to appreciate not only Chinese culture but also the Chinese lifestyle; and how through hard work and energy this community has laid down roots for the future in British life. We hope that young people, both Chinese and non-Chinese, will make friends and learn to understand each other better.

Further Reading

BASIC READING

- D.C. Money : <u>China Today</u> (Cambridge U. Press 1987)

- Anthony Shang : <u>Living in Hong Kong</u> (Macdonald 1984)

- Richard Newnham : <u>About Chinese</u> (Penguin 1971)

- Straits Times Collection : <u>Fun with Chinese characters</u> (Federal Publications 1980)

- Anthony Shang : <u>Chinese in Britain</u> (Macdonald 1984)

- Hugh Baker : <u>The Overseas Chinese</u> (Batsford 1987)

- Lip Evelyn : <u>Chinese Temples and Deities</u> (Times Book International 1981)

- Raymond Dawson : <u>Confucius</u> (Oxford U. Press 1981)

- J.C. Cooper : <u>Taoism</u> (Aquarian Press 1972)

- Guanghwa Co. : <u>Introduction to popular traditions and customs of the Chinese New Year</u> (Guanghwa Co. 1986)

MORE SPECIALISED MATERIAL

- The Runneymede Trust : <u>The Chinese Community in Britain - Home Office Committee Report in Context</u> (Runneymede Trust 1985)

- Monica Taylor : <u>Chinese pupils in Britain</u> (NFER-Nelson 1987)

- Hong Kong Urban Council : <u>Hong Kong One Hundred Years Ago</u> (Hong Kong 1970)

- Smith-Wesley : <u>Unequal Treaty 1898-1997 : China, Great Britain and Hong Kong's New Territories</u> (Oxford U. Press 1980)

- Kaplan and Sobin : <u>Encyclopedia of China Today</u> (Macmillan 1982)

- V.R. Burkhardt : <u>Chinese Creeds and Customs</u> (S.C.M.P. 1982)

- Qi Xing : <u>Folk Customs at traditional Chinese festivals</u> (Foreign Language Press 1988)

- Jonathan Chamberlain : <u>Chinese Gods</u> (Pelanduk Publications 1987)

- China Handbook Series : <u>Life and Lifestyles</u> (Foreign Language Press 1985)

- J.M. Kermadec : <u>The Way to Chinese Astrology</u> (Unwin Paperbacks 1983)

- De Francis : <u>The Chinese Language - Fact and Fantasy</u> (University of Hawaii Press 1984)

- Julian Schutski : <u>Research on the I Ching</u> (Routledge and Kegan Paul 1980)

A BRIEF CHINESE CHRONOLOGY

夏　　XIA: ....c. 21st C. BC to c. 16th C. BC

商　　SHANG: ....c. 16th C. BC to c. 11th C. BC

西周　WESTERN ZHOU: ....c. 11th C. BC to year 771 BC

東周　EASTERN ZHOU
      Spring and Autumn Period: ....770 BC to 476 BC
      Warring States period: ....475 BC to 221 BC

秦　　QIN/CHIN: ....221 BC to 207 BC

西漢　WESTERN HAN: ....206 BC to AD 25

東漢　EASTERN HAN: ....AD 25 to 220

三國　THREE KINGDOMS (Wei, Shu and Wu): ....220 to 265

西晉　WESTERN JIN: ....265 to 316

東晉　EASTERN JIN: ....317 to 420

南北朝　SOUTHERN AND NORTHERN: ....420 to 580

隋　　SUI: ....581 to 618

唐　　TANG: ....618 to 907

[五代十國　FIVE DYNASTIES AND TEN KINGDOMS: ....907 to 960

南北宋　NORTHERN AND SOUTHERN SUNG: ....960 to 1279

元　　YUAN: ....1279 to 1368

明　　MING: ....1368 to 1644

清　　QING/CHING: ....1644 to 1911

中華民國　THE FIRST REPUBLIC: ....1912 to 1949

中華人民共和國　THE PEOPLE'S REPUBLIC: ....1949 to the present day

      • Please note that on October 1 every year the
People's Republic of China celebrates her National Day.

Appendix 2

THE CHINESE CALENDAR

The old Chinese calendar governs the cultural, festive, religious and spiritual life of most Chinese people.

The Chinese calendar is a lunar one, being made up of 12 lunar months of 29 to 30 days each. As the lunar year is shorter than the solar year of 365 days, what is called an intercalary month is added to every four years to keep the lunar and solar calendars roughly parallel. This intercalary month must be inserted seven times every nineteen years, in such a way that the winter solstice (December 21 in our calendar) will always fall in the eleventh month, the summer solstice (June 22 in our calendar) in the fifth, the spring equinox (March 21 in our calendar) in the second and the autumn equinox (September 21 in our calendar) in the eighth month. It does not come as an extra month at the end of the year, but is simply inserted between two other months, so that during a year when it occurs there may be two successive fifth, sixth or other two months, as the course may be, following one another. The first and the twelfth month cannot be re-duplicated in this way, however.

This calendric system has remained unchanged since its reform about two thousand years ago, during the Han Dynasty. According to this system, the Chinese New Year Day has been arranged to fall not before January 21 and not later than February 20.

• Remember that if your birthday is in April, then according to the Chinese calendar you were born in March.

THE CHINESE ZODIAC

The Chinese zodiac is divided into 12 yearly cycles.
Each of the 12 years is named after an animal.

Name of Year	Past and Future Dates					
HORSE:	1954	1966	1978	1990	2002	2014
SHEEP:	1955	1967	1979	1991	2003	2015
MONKEY:	1956	1968	1980	1992	2004	2016
COCK:	1957	1969	1981	1993	2005	2017
DOG:	1958	1970	1982	1994	2006	2018
PIG:	1959	1971	1983	1995	2007	2019
RAT:	1960	1972	1984	1996	2008	2020
OX:	1961	1973	1985	1997	2009	2021
TIGER:	1962	1974	1986	1998	2010	2022
RABBIT:	1963	1975	1987	1999	2011	2023
DRAGON:	1964	1976	1988	2000	2012	2024
SNAKE:	1965	1977	1989	2001	2013	2025

Appendix 4

SOME SIMPLE CHINESE DELICACIES

1) Yang Chow Fried Rice

Legend has it that the Emperor of China, who had to travel around in disguise for his own safety, arrived late one night in the city of Yang Chow. The only dish that could be prepared for him was a fry-up of the day's left-overs. He found it so delicious that he named it Yang Chow Fried Rice. This dish is very popular in Chinese restaurants and take-aways all over the U.K.

Ingredients - *for four people*

2 eggs

2 spring onions

2 tablespoons of oil

Half teaspoon salt

4 oz. bacon, cut into pieces

4 oz. frozen prawns (cooked and peeled)

2 oz. frozen peas

1 lb. cooked, boiled long grain white rice

Method

1) Finely chop the spring onions.

2) Beat the eggs, and add salt.

3) Heat the wok, and pour in one tablespoon of oil.

4) When the oil is hot, pour in the egg. Then turn it once, like an omelette. Remove it from oil and keep it on a side plate.

5) Add the remaining oil, fry the bacon, add the peas and prawns, and stir fry. Turn the heat down. Add the fried egg and beat it into small pieces.

6) Add the cooked, boiled rice to the mixture. Make sure that the rice is not too hot before you add it. Next add the chopped spring onions. The fried rice is now ready to serve.

2) Sweet and Sour Soup

This very tasty soup dish is from the Sichuan province of China. It too is highly popular in Britain.

Ingredients - *for four people*

4 oz. lean pork or minced meat

1 square beancurd, (tofu)

4 oz. sliced mushrooms

1 tablespoon of soya sauce

Half teaspoon of chilli powder

1 tablespoon of vinegar

2 teaspoons of cornflour

1 teaspoon salt

1 cube of chicken stock

1 teaspoon of sesame oil

2 tablespoons of sugar

One and a half pints of water

Method

1) Boil the water, and add the pork or meat, mushrooms, beancurd and chicken stock. Bring the water back to boiling point, and then let it simmer for about 5 minutes.·

2) Add soya sauce, chilli powder, sugar, vinegar and cornflour solution (made by mixing cornflour with 1 tablespoon of cold water).

3) Cook until the soup thickens, and then add salt and sesame oil.

3) Vegetarian Spring Rolls

Spring rolls were eaten as part of the New Year spring festival. Now they are eaten throughout the year as a Dim Sum delicacy. Again they are very popular with the British diners. In some take-aways they are called Chop Suey Rolls.

Ingredients

A medium sized packet of spring roll pastry

1 lb. of beansprouts or 8 oz. of shredded white cabbage

4 oz. carrots or bamboo shoots

2 oz. mushrooms

About a mug of corn oil for frying

2 teaspoons of corn starch

1 teaspoon salt

1 teaspoon sugar

Method

1) Peel and shred carrots, shred the bamboo shoots and slice the mushrooms.

2) Lightly saute bean sprouts or cabbage in a little oil.

3) Heat pan with oil again and add mushrooms, carrots or bamboo shoots, bean sprouts or cabbage, sugar and salt. Let the vegetables cook.

4) Put pastry flat on the table, add 2 tablespoons of vegetable filling, and roll towards the centre. But please make sure that the filling is properly cooled and that the excess water has been drained away before filling the pastry. Use corn starch solution (made by mixing corn starch with a little water) to seal the pastry.

5) Pour all the remaining oil in the frying pan or wok, dip the spring rolls in hot oil, and deep fry them until golden brown.

4) Prawn Crackers

Traditionally prawn crackers have been eaten at times of celebration. The cracking of the crackers, as they are eaten, reminds people of happiness. Now they are regularly served in Chinese restaurants and take-aways and eaten as snacks.

Buy a packet of dried prawn crackers from a Chinese supermarket. Heat some oil in a wok, and deep fry the prawn crackers for about one minute. In order to make sure that the oil is not too hot or too cold, dip just one prawn cracker for testing. It should be crispy and white in colour.

If you are frying a large quantity, take care to keep the oil clear. It should not look too browned or burnt.

All of the ingredients in these menus are available from Chinese supermarkets throughout Britain. Many of them can also be bought in your local large supermarket.

HOW TO USE CHOPSTICKS

The Chinese may have been the first people in the world to stop using hands to eat. They invented a versatile tool called a chopstick. You normally hold two chopsticks together.

1 Place the first chopstick in the hollow between thumb and index finger and rest its lower end below the first joint of the third finger. This chopstick remains stationary.

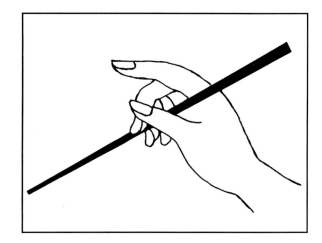

2 Hold the other chopstick between the tips of the index and middle fingers, steady its upper half against the base of the index finger, and use the tip of the thumb to keep it in place.

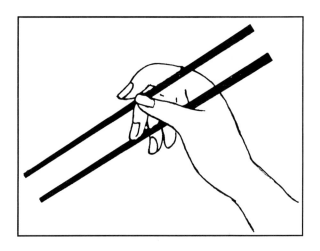

3 To pick up things, move the upper chopsticks with index and middle fingers.

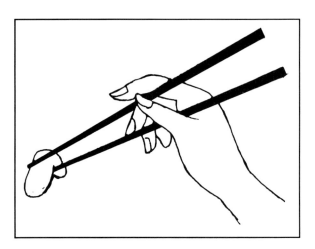

THE IMPERIAL ARCH IN THE MANCHESTER CHINATOWN

The famous Chinese Arch of Manchester was built during 1987 and 1988. Many people and organisations helped to build it. It is designed in the style of the Ching Dynasty, and it is one of the only two authentic arches outside China. The other is in Sydney, Australia, which like Manchester is a Dragon City.

The total cost of building the Arch was £350,000. The Chinese Government contributed most, £105,000, and Chinese craftsmen were specially brought over from China, and they brought with them the ceramics for external surfacing and the stone carving slabs. The Chinese community of Manchester raised £65,000, while other large sums were donated by the Department of Environment, the Greater Manchester Council and the Manchester City Council.

The Arch gives great dignity to Manchester Chinatown. Many visitors to Manchester come to see it and are much impressed by its size, design and decoration.

Appendix 6

A LIST OF SOME INTERESTING TRADITIONAL CHINESE STORIES FOR CHILDREN

Some Children's Classics - Compulsory for Chinese children

1) ### A Dream of Red Mansions, *by TSAO, Hseueh - Chin*

   This is a classical novel written in the mid eighteenth century. It is a story about class struggles between the rich and the poor during the period of Chinese feudalism. The last feudal dynasty in China was the Ching dynasty.

2) ### Romance of the Three Kingdoms, *by LO Kuan - Chung*

   This book is regarded by the Chinese as their greatest novel and is a product of the 14th century. Based on historical fact, it portrays human ambition against a background of adventure and intrigue.

3) ### Outlaws of the Marsh, *by LUO Guan - Zhong*

   This adventure story is set in the final years of a Sung emperor, Hui Zhong, who reigned from 1101 to 1125. It describes the adventures of a hundred women who became leaders of an outlaw army of thousands in the Sandong Province and how they fought battles against the heartless tyrants. (BBC TV has previously shown this story under the name of "Water Margin").

4) ### Journey to the West, *by WU Cheng - En*

   This is another famous adventure story. Chinese children adore the so-called Monkey King who is the chief character in the story. Based on traditional folktale from the Ming dynasty, the story is a fantasy which relates the adventures of a Tang dynasty priest and his three disciples who travel west (ie. to India) in search of the Buddhist sutra.

5) ### Romances of the West Chamber, *by WANG Shi - Po*

   This is a classical story to describe the emotions of a young Chinese person's love and the pressure from the arranged feudal marriage. It tells us about the importance of the role of a match maker.

Some Legends

6) ### Shen Nong's Miracle Herbs

   This story, highly recommended for children aged ten and above, is based on an ancient Chinese legend about a man named Shen Nong who cured people's illnesses by using herbal medicines.

7) ### Kua Fu races with the Sun

   This is a folk story based on the legend of the beginning of the Sun and how Kua Fu made the sun rise and set everyday on time.

8) ### Hou Yu shoots the Suns

   This is another legendary folk story. It is related to the mid-autumn festival and to the belief in a moon fairy. Highly popular in the Chinese sunday schools, it is read a lot to the children.

A CROSSWORD PUZZLE

Across

1 Capital of China

3 A mythological animal - symbol of China

6 The Master Teacher

9 Pot for storing the relics of ancestors

10 A busy day in a chinatown

11 China is to the —— of Britain

13 The biggest city in the south of China (now known as Guangzhou)

15 Chinese people or Chinese dynasty

16 An indoor game for four people

18 A martial art

20 Needed for a famous Chinese outdoor hobby

22 One of the animal signs in the Chinese horoscope

23 First Communist leader of China

24 Present spoken language of China (Modern Chinese language)

Down

1 A feast

2 Burnt for pleasant smell during worship

4 A Chinese classical, musical play

5 Chinese word for longevity

7 Exploded on festival days

8 Traditional heir to the family

12 A British city with the oldest chinatown

14 An appetizer

15 Original settlers in Hong Kong

17 The Cantonese word for the Chinese language

19 Chinese word for rice

21 First grown in China

Exercise 2

PREPARING FOR A TRIP TO HONG KONG

If you are thinking of going to Hong Kong as a tourist, make sure that you have the correct answers to the questions set out in the checklist below. This exercise is intended to initiate investigation outside of the classroom. There may be several solutions to the questions set.

Passport :

1) Have you got a valid passport?
2) If the answer to No. 1) is "No", where would you have to apply for a passport?
3) Do you need a visa to go to Hong Kong?
4) If the answer to No. 3) is "Yes", where would you have to apply for a visa?

Air Ticket :

1) Where would you buy your air ticket from?
2) By which airline are you hoping to travel?
3) What is the fare? Can you afford it?
4) Have you inquired about the fares of other airline companies?
5) Who can help you to choose the airline with the right fare for you?

Currency :

1) What is the currency used in Hong Kong?
2) What is the rate of exchange between Hong Kong currency and the British currency?
3) How much money are you able to afford on this trip?
4) How would you decide whether the amount of money you are taking with you will be enough for the trip?
5) How will you take your money with you? Will it all be in the form of cash?

Hotel :

1) Where would you get the list of Hong Kong hotels?
2) How would you reserve a hotel booking for yourself?
3) What type of hotel would you prefer?
4) What would you do if you have not got enough money to afford to stay in the hotel that you prefer?

Places of interest

1) Do you know which places in Hong Kong you particularly wish to see?
2) If the answer to No. 1) is "No", how would you find out about the interesting places?
3) In order not to get lost in Hong Kong what would you need to take with you or buy there as soon as you arrive?

Weather

1) Which is the best time of the year to go to Hong Kong?
2) How hot does Hong Kong get? Do you like hot weather?
3) What precautions do you need to take to be sure that too much heat does not upset you?
4) When is the rainy season in Hong Kong?

Time difference

1) What is the difference in time between Hong Kong and Britain?

2) When does your flight start from Britain, and at what time does it arrive at Hong Kong? How many hours' journey is that?

3) When does your return flight from Hong Kong start, and at what time does your plane arrive in Britain? How many hours' journey is the return flight?

4) Is there any difference in the time taken by the outward flight and the return flight?

Luggage

1) What are the main items of clothing you need on your trip?

2) Do you need to carry any medicines?

3) What other personal items would you like to take with you?

4) Besides what you took with you, what would you have in your luggage on your return flight? Why?

Food

1) Do you like Chinese food?

2) Which dishes are you looking forward to having in Hong Kong?

3) Do you think it is possible to have an English dish like Roast Beef and Yorkshire Pudding or any other of your favourite dishes in Hong Kong?

Language

1) What is the main Chinese dialect spoken in Hong Kong?

2) Do you think there would be much English spoken in Hong Kong?

3) What would you take with you to help you to communicate with the Chinese people who do not speak English?

A TRIP INTO CHINATOWN

It is just after 11.00 am on a Sunday morning and the Wong family set off from the outskirts of Manchester to visit Chinatown. They like to get there early as parking can be a big problem.

When they arrive Mr Wong drops his daughter off at the Chinese Sunday School. Then he goes to get a haircut. He gets his hair cut only in Chinatown as he believes the Chinese barber knows Chinese hair and he can also communicate better in Chinese. Meanwhile Mrs Wong, her son and her mother-in-law go to a restaurant to "Yam Char". There they meet up with friends. Mr Wong comes to join them after his haircut. They order dimsum, including beef rice roll (Cheung Fan), steamed prawn and meat ball (Siu Mai), steamed prawn dumpling (Har Gau), braised chicken claw (Fung Tzau, meaning phoenix feet), deep fried prawn parcel (Won Ton).

After about an hour and a half the meal finishes and Mr Wong goes to collect his daughter from the Sunday School. Mrs Wong goes with her son to the bakery and the Chinese supermarket. It is her son's birthday and at the bakery she buys a Hong Kong style birthday cake and some smaller buns. At the supermarket she looks for ingredients to make spring rolls. She buys Chinese pancake pastry and some beansprouts, along with some fresh ginger and spring onions.

Mrs Wong's mother-in-law goes to buy joss sticks from the arts and craft shop before going with a friend to the jewellers to look at some jade. Mrs Wong's daughter has gone to another art shop to buy the "Oriental Sunday" and "Fresh Weekly", two Hong Kong weekly magazines, and a couple of CDs of Canto Pop stars. Her father comes into the shop to buy a lucky charm to hang from the mirror in the car and a Chinese newspaper.

Finally, after several stops along the way to chat to friends, the Wongs go back to the car. Before setting off for home Mr Wong drives to the supermarket to buy a 100 lb. sack of rice which the porter puts into their car boot. They arrive back at the take-away at about 4.30 pm, in time to prepare for the evening opening.

QUESTIONS

1   **What are Chinese Sunday Schools for?**

2   **Mr Wong has two reasons why he likes to have his hair cut at the Chinese hairdressers. What are they?**

3   **What is "Yam Char"? How are dimsums generally brought to your table in a restaurant? Make a list of as many dimsums that you can find in Chinese restaurants.**

4   **What is the use of joss sticks?**

5   **Why is jade in such great demand in the Chinatown jewellery shops?**

6   **What do you think Mrs Wong's daughter may expect to read in the Hong Kong weekly magazines?**

7   **Why does Mr Wong buy so much rice on one trip?**

MAKING A CHINESE NEW YEAR CARD

You can make your own Chinese New Year cards. Use nice and colourful cards of A4 size; gently fold them into two halves, and write your own message or wish inside. Pictures may also be drawn and colourful Chinese calligraphic writing can be very exciting.

The illustration below on the left is typical of what you may see on the front of the cards, and you can draw similarly, using your own imagination and drawing style. On the right are four usual messages and wishes. You may expand the calligraphy and present them colourfully.

出入平安 — BLESSED WITH PEACE AND SAFETY

從心所欲 — ALL WISHES COME TRUE

大吉大利 — GOOD LUCK AND GOOD FORTUNE

一本萬利 — MAY YOUR BUSINESS PROSPER

IMAGINATIVE WRITING

Try to complete the following three stories. The first two stories help to start you off, while in the third story you have to lead up to the ending that is written for you.

I go to sleep very late

I live with my mother, father, brother and sister in a take-away shop about six to seven miles from Manchester's Chinatown. My father started the take-away some years ago when we were still very young. Both my father and mother work very hard in the kitchen. As I am the eldest child my parents expect me to help...... *COMPLETE THE STORY.*

The big black egg

A long time ago the heaven and the earth were all one and there was only chaos. From the big, black egg there appeared a giant. Or what is it the Goddess Nu Wa? Whether it was the giant or the goddess, something strange was about to happen on this earth. For millions of years the earth had remained empty. There were no people. Now in China all this was to change....... *COMPLETE THE STORY.*

What a great day!

START THE STORY HERE AND FINISH WITH THE FOLLOWING ENDING....... The long evening was drawing to a close. What wonderful memories have I of the whole day that began at six in the morning and that is now slowly coming to an end. One last bang of balloons would bring everyone out. And then all of us can go home and get to bed. Sweet dreams, and roll on next year's Chinese New Year party.

YOU MAY HAVE MORE IDEAS OF YOUR OWN FOR WRITING AN IMAGINARY STORY AFTER READING OUR BOOK.

MAP KNOWLEDGE QUESTIONS

1) At the beginning of this century people travelled mostly by sea between Hong Kong and Britain. The liners had two routes to follow. They would first sail to Singapore, and then they could either branch out to Bombay for a journey through the Red Sea, Suez Canal and the Mediterranean Sea, or they could sail down to Cape Town in South Africa and then take the Atlantic Ocean route to Britain.

On Map 1 draw both sea routes. Also on the map fill in Atlantic Ocean, Pacific Ocean and the Indian Ocean.

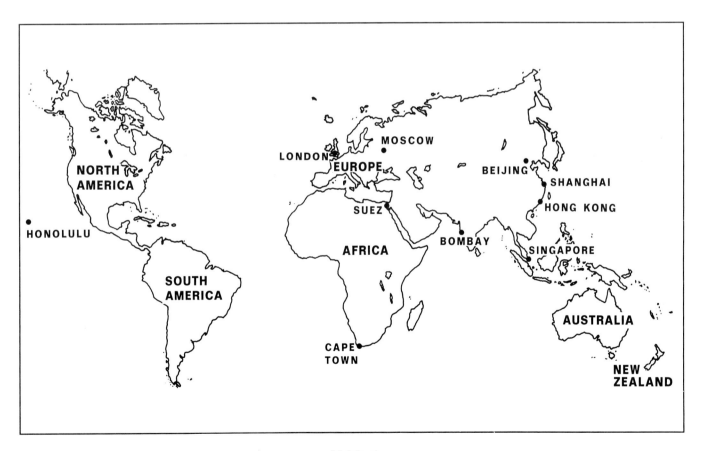

MAP 1

2) Map 1 is a very simple way of drawing the shape of the earth on a flat surface. It is important to remember, however, that the earth is not flat but spherical. It is like a ball. Another way of mapping the earth is to see it as a globe. Map 2 below does that for you.

Nowadays people mostly travel by air. On Map 2 draw two different air routes between Hong Kong and London : one via Shanghai, Beijing and Moscow, and the other via Singapore and Bombay.

Someone travelling from Hong Kong to London first wants to visit Honolulu in the Hawaii Islands. Draw on Map 2 the route that will be taken.

MAP 2

3) In the map below put crosses to indicate the following cities in Britain where there are a number of Chinese settled.

London, Liverpool, Manchester, Leeds, Sheffield, Glasgow, Edinburgh, Stirling, Belfast, Cardiff, Newcastle, Birmingham.

MAP 3

Although the following contact addresses and telephone numbers were correct at the time of publication, they may be subject to change. Also some new organisations may be founded whilst others may cease to operate.

EMBASSIES AND CONSULATES

The Embassy of the People's Republic of China

49-51 Portland Place
London
W1N 3AH
Tel: 0171 636 0288

Consulate of the People's Republic of China

Denison House, Denison Road
Victoria Park, Rusholme
Manchester
M14 5 RX
Tel: 0161 224 7480

The Hong Kong Government Office

6 Grafton Street
London
W1X 3LB
Tel: 0171 499 9821

Taipei Representative Office in the UK

50 Grosvenor Gardens
London
SW1W 0EB
Tel: 0171 396 9152

CHINESE CENTRES AND ORGANISATIONS

London

Chinese Chamber of Commerce UK

19-20 Frith Street

London WC2

Tel: 0191 200 3409 or 0171 734 8135

Kung Ho Association

9 Kenrick Place

London

W14 3FF

Tel: 0171 487 4573

Charing Cross Library (Chinese Section)

Westminster

London

Tel: 0171 798 2058 or 0171 798 2053

Guanghwa Book Shop

China Art Cultural Centre

32 Parker Street

Covent Garden, London

WC2B 5PH

Tel: 0171 831 5888

The Society for Anglo-Chinese Understanding

152 Camden High Street

London NW1

Tel: 0171 485 8236 or 081 202 5297

BBC World Service Chinese Section

Room 125NE Bush House

The Strand

London

WC2B 4PH

Tel: 0171 240 3456 Ext 3087

CNE Chinese Channel

Chinese News and Entertainment

Sky Sports 2

47 Station

London

Tel: 0171 610 3880

Spectrum Radio

PO Box 5000

Brent Cross

London

NW2 1JT

Tel: 0181 905 5000

Waltham Forest Chinese Association

Greater London House

547-551 High Road

Leytonstone

London E11

Tel: 0181 558 0182

Directory of Chinese Organisations

The Great Britain China Centre

15 Belgrave Square

London

SW1X 8PG

Tel: 0171 235 9216

Chinese Catering Association

C/o 29 Kensington High Street

London

W8 5NP

Tel: 0171 494 2412 or 0171 494 1230

London Chinese Lutheran Church

The American Church

79 Tottenham Court Road

London W1

Tel: 0171 383 2964

Haringey Chinese Association

211 Langham Road

London N15 3LH

Tel: 0181 881 8649

Brent Chinese Association

31 First Avenue

Wembley

Middlesex

HA9 8QG

Tel: 0181 908 1233 or 0181 952 4701

Camden Chinese Community Centre

173 Arlington Road

Camden Town

London

NW1 7EY

Tel: 0171 267 3019

Westminster Chinese Community Centre

2nd Floor

44 Gerard Street

London WC2

Tel: 0171 439 3822

Chinese Catering Association

C/o 15 Little Newport Street

London WC2

Chinese Information and Advice Centre

2nd Floor 68 Shaftesbury Ave

London WC2H 8HL

Tel: 0171 836 8291 or 0171 494 3273

Greenwich Chinese Community Association

141 Greenwich High Road

Greenwich SE10

Tel: 0181 858 2410

Hackney Chinese Community Service

28 Ellingford Road

London

E8 3PA

Tel: 0181 986 6171

Lambeth Chinese Community Association

69 Stockwell Road

London

SW9 9PY

Tel: 0171 733 4377 or 0171 738 4589

London Chinese Health Resource Centre

43 Dean Street

London WC2

Tel: 0171 287 0904

Chinese Association of Tower Hamlets

680 Commercial Road

Sailor's Place

London

E14 7HA

Tel: 0161 515 5598 or 0171 554 5091

Newham Chinese Association

Room 8

Park House

64 West Ham Lane

London

E15 4PT

Tel: 0181 519 8949 or 0181 519 6488

Manchester

Chinese Library

Manchester Central Library

St Peter's Square

Manchester

M2 5PD

Tel: 0161 234 1970

Manchester Master Chu Lion Dancing Group

110 Portland Street

Manchester

0161 236 3933

Manchester Chinese Chamber of Commerce

George Street

Manchester

Tel: 0161 928 4523

Chinese Advisory Centre

101 Portland Street

Manchester

North West Overseas Chinese Association

Nicholas Street

Manchester Chinatown

Tel: 0161 228 3648

Ng Yip Association (UK)

C/o 16 Nicholas Street

Manchester

Tel: 0161 228 7871 or 0161 881 9713

Wu Kan Tang Overseas Chinese Association Nicholas Street

Manchester Chinatown

Tel: 0161 653 9449 or 0161 236 7003

Manchester Chinese Cultural Educational

and Community Centre

61 Dickenson Street

Manchester

Tel: 0161 228 3926

Directory of Chinese Organisations

Chinese Arts Centre

36 Charlotte Street

Manchester M1

Tel: 0161 236 9251

Eastern Horizon (GMR)

C/o New Broadcasting House

PO Box 90

Oxford Road

Manchester

M60 1SJ

Tel: 0161 200 2000

Buddhist Light International Association (BLIA)

110 Portland Street

Manchester

Tel: 0161 236 0494

Manchester Chinese Christian Fellowship

100 Yarburgh Street

Whalley Range

Manchester

Tel: 0161 226 5831 or 0161 862 6796

Chinese Art Association

C/o T La Art and Gallery

Nicholas Street

Manchester Chinatown

Tel: 0161 273 2918

Chinese Health Information Centre

6 Houldsworth Street

Manchester M1 1EJ

Tel: 0161 228 0138

Liverpool

The Pagoda of Hundred Harmony

(The Chinese Community Centre)

Henry Street

Liverpool L1 5BU

Tel: 0151 708 8833

Silk Road News

Room 29

The Royal Institution

Colquitt Street

Liverpool L1 4DE

Tel: 0151 709 2359

See Yap Chinese Association

22 Nelson Street

Liverpool L1

Tel: 0151 709 1605

Liverpool Chinese Gospel Church

19-20 Great George Square

Liverpool L1

Tel: 0151 487 3927

Wah Sing Chinese Community Centre

149 Duke Street

Liverpool L1

Tel: 0151 709 4609 or Sunday 1.30-6.00 pm

Mr Cheung 0151 709 9842

Oriental Express

BBC

Liverpool

Tel: 0151 708 5500

Leeds

Wah Kwong Chinese Association

10 Barwick Road

Leeds 15

Birmingham

Birmingham Chinese Association

Unit 1

96 Coventry Street

Birmingham

B5 5NY

Sheffield

Sheffield Chinese Christian Church

C/o Watson Road

Broomhill

Sheffield

S10 2SD

Leicester

Chinese Community Centre

170A Belgrave Gate

Leicester

LE1 3XL

Leicester Chinese Association

C/o 5 Melton Street

Leicester

LE1 3NA

Directory of Chinese Organisations

Wales

Cardiff Chinese Community Services
Cathedral Road
Cardiff
CF1 9PP

Lam Chuen Overseas Chinese Community Association
112 St David's Road
Aberravenny
Gwent
South Wales

Scotland

Confederation of Chinese Associations of Scotland
15 Hyndford Place
Dundee
Scotland
DD1 1SH

Chinese Newspapers Published in UK (National Paper)

Sing Tao Newspaper UK Ltd
46 Denn Street
London
Tel: 0171 287 1525

Si Yu Chinese Times
16, Nicholas Street
Manchester
M1
Tel: 0161 228 0240

Wen Wei Po
11 Little Newport Street
London
Tel: 0171 734 2144/5

Directory of Chinese Schools

Name of School and Place	Telephone	Day & hours of opening
The London Area		
Chinese Chamber of Commerce UK Chinese School London W1	0181 200 3409	9.30am - 6 pm (Sat & Sun)
Kung Ho Association Chinese School	0181 487 4573	11am - 3.30pm (Sun)
Overseas Chinese Education Centre Hounslow	01628 37773	10.30am - 12.30pm (Sat) Schs 1, 3 & 4, Sch 2 11am - 1pm (Sat)
Overseas Chinese Education Centre London NW1		10.30am - 12.30pm (Sat) Schs 1, 3 & 4, ch 2 11am - 1pm (Sat)
Overseas Chinese Education Centre London WC2		10.30am - 12.30pm (Sat) Schs 1, 3 & 4, Sch 2 11am - 1pm (Sat)
St Martin-in-the Fields Church Chinese Congregation London WC2	01226 730914	1.45 - 2.30pm (Sun)
Rhenish Church (UK) Ltd., Chinese Class London WC2	0181 965 4140	12.30 - 1.30pm (Sun)
Ming Dak Chinese School London WC2	01923-534275 (Home) 0181 450 8911 Ext 205 (Day)	12 noon - 3pm (Sun)
Harrow Chinese School Harrow, Middx	0181 907 0827	2.30 - 4.30pm (Sat)
Pastor Stephen Wang Memorial Chinese Class London N7	0181 989 9873	10am - 12.30pm (Sat)
True Jesus Church (London) London N1	0181 802 8531	2pm (Sat)
Qing Hau Chinese School West Harrow, Middx	0181 861 4983	10am - 12 noon (Sat)
Qing Hau Chinese School Wembley, Middx		10am - 3pm (Sun)
Qing Hau Chinese School Ealing		2pm - 4pm (Sat)
Ealing Chinese (Mandarin) School Acton W3	0181 992 2562	10am - 12.30pm (Sat)
Walthamstow Forest Chinese Association School Walthamstow E17	0181 558 0182	1.15 - 3.30pm (Sun)
Brent Chinese Association London NW10	0181 952 4701	10.30am - 12.30pm (Sun)
Haringey Chinese Association Chinese Class London N17	0181 881 8649	10am - 4pm (Sat)

Directory of Chinese Schools

Name of School	Telephone	Day & hours of opening
Hackney Chinese Community Services - Mother Tongue Class London E2	0171 729 7145	10am - 12 noon (Sat)
Chinese Association of Tower Hamlets London E3	0171 554 5091	10am - 12 noon (Sat)
Chum Yee Chinese School (Society) London E14	0181 987 1872	1 - 3.30pm (Sun)
Lambeth Chinese Community School London SW8	0171 733 4377 or 0171 738 4589	10am - 2pm (Sat)
Balham Chinese School Balham SW12	Chestnut Grove School Boundaries Rd London SW12	10.30am - 12.30pm (Sat)
Greenwich Chinese Community School Greenwich SE10	0181 858 2410	10.30am - 3pm (Sun) 1 - 4pm (Sat)
Pei Hua Chinese School London W5	0181 550 2023	10am - 1pm (Sat)
Newham Chinese Association on Chinese Class London E6	0181 534 0683	2 - 4pm (Sat)
Light & Love Chinese School London SW2	0181 674 8223	

The North West

Manchester Chinese Christian Church Sunday School Manchester	0161 862 6796	10.30am - 12.30pm (Sun)
North West Chinese Language School Manchester	0161 440 8473	1 - 4pm (Sun)
Manchester Chinese Education Culture & Community Centre Chinese School Manchester	0161 330 1456 or 864 3825	1.45 - 4.30 pm (Sat) 11.45am - 2.20pm (Sun)
Wah Sing Chinese Community Centre Chinese School Liverpool	0151 709 4609	2 - 4.15pm (Sun)
Liverpool Chinese Gospel Church Chinese Class Liverpool	0151 487 3927	2.30 - 4pm (Sat)
Preston Chinese Christian Sunday School Preston, Lancashire	01772 612458 (after 4pm)	1.30 - 3.40pm (Sun)

The North East

Newcastle Upon Tyne Chinese School Newcastle Upon Tyne	0191 222 6214	1 - 5pm (Sun)
True Jesus Church Newcastle Chinese Class Newcastle Upon Tyne	0191 263 7756 (H) 0191 261 5787 (W)	12.15 - 3.15 pm (Sun)
North East Chinese School (UK) Middlesbrough, Cleveland	01642 761216	3 - 5.30pm (Sun)

Directory of Chinese Schools

Name of School and Place	Telephone	Day & hours of opening
Yorkshire		
Leeds & District Chinese Community Word Understanding Class Leeds	01532 755905	2 - 4pm (Sun)
Yuk Wah School Leeds	01943 816287	2 - 4pm (Sun)
Leeds Chinese Christian Fellowship Chinese Class Leeds	01532 755905	2 - 4.15pm (Sat)
Hull Chinese Class Hull	01482 799202	2 - 4pm (Sun)
Sheffield & District Association Chinese School Sheffield	01532 336496 (Day)	2 - 4.20pm (Sun)
Sheffield Chinese Christian Church Sheffield	01742 685902	11.30 - 1.30pm (Sun)
Huddersfield Chinese Centre Huddersfield	01484 517113	1.30 - 3pm (Sat)
The West Yorks Chinese Community Association Chinese School Bradford	01535 274611	Sunday
Doncaster Chinese School Association Doncaster	01302 370215	
Grimsby Chinese Community Word Understanding Class Grimsby	01472 752008	2 - 5pm (Sun)
Scunthorpe Chinese Community Word Understanding Class Scunthorpe	01724 860202	2 - 4pm (Sun)
West Midlands & Staffordshire		
Overseas Chinese Association Chinese School Birmingham	0121 637 2720 (Day)	1.30 - 3.30pm (Sun)
Birmingham Chinese School Birmingham	0121 449 1678	10.30am - 12.30pm & 1 - 3pm (Sat)
In Memorial of Pastor Stephen Wang Chinese Class Birmingham	0121 427 4907	10.30 - 12.30pm (Sat)
Chinese Community (Coventry) Association Chinese Class Coventry	01203 433067	2 - 4pm (Sun)
Staffordshire Chinese Community Association Chinese Class Stoke-on-Trent	01782 711637	1.30 - 3.30pm (Sun)

Directory of Chinese Schools

Name of School and Place	Telephone	Day & hours of opening
East Midlands		
Derbyshire Chinese Welfare Derby	013317 3129 & 01332 42436	2 - 4pm (Sun)
True Jesus Church (Leicester) Chinese Association Leicester	01533 767319	3 - 4pm (Sun)
Leicester Chinese Christian Fellowship Chinese Class Leicester	01533 880689	2.30 - 4.30pm (Sun)
East England Chinese Association School Nottingham	01602 298057	2 - 4pm (Sun)
Home Counties		
Banbury School Chinese Class Banbury	01295 267332	10am - 12 noon (Sat)
Cambridge Chinese Class Cambridge	01223 441071	1 - 4pm (Sun)
Bedfordshire Chinese School Luton, Beds	01582 422499	12 noon - 2pm (Sun)
Bedfordshire & Luton Chinese Educational and Cultural Association Luton, Beds	01582 571132	12.45 - 2.45pm (Sun)
Milton Keynes Chinese School Milton Keynes	01908 677381	10am - 12.15pm (Sun)
Northampton Chinese Language School Northampton	01604 765251	12.30 - 2.30pm (Sun)
Oxford Chinese Christian Church Chinese Class Oxford	01865 65756	1.45 - 2.45pm (Sun)
Oxford Chinese Class Oxford	018675 863989	1 - 5pm (Sun)
Hertfordshire Chinese Tuition Stevenage, Herts	01438 367240	11am - 1pm (Sun)
Wales and South West		
Bristol Chinese Language Class Bristol	01272 682340	2 - 4pm (Sun)
Overseas Chinese Association, Bristol Chinese Language Class Bristol	01272 240797	2 - 4pm (Sun)
Cardiff Chinese Christian Fellowship Sunday School Cardiff	01222 761366	2.30 - 4.30pm (Sun)
South Wales Chinese School Cardiff	01222 777441	2 - 4pm (Sun)

Directory of Chinese Schools

Name of School and Place	Telephone	Day & hours of opening
Devon & Cornwall (P) Chinese Association Sunday Class Plymouth	01752 367426	1 - 4pm (Sun)
Devon & Cornwall (C) Chinese Association Sunday Class Cornwall	0209 719955	12.30 - 3.30pm (Sun)
Gloucester Chinese Class Gloucester	01452 414101 or 424723	12 noon - 2pm (Sun)

South and Sout East

Brighton Chinese Sunday School Sussex	01273 680737	1 - 3pm (Sun)
Kent Chinese Class Canterbury, Kent	01227 76400	1.30 - 3.30pm (Sun)
Kut O Chinese Association Chatham, Kent	01634 846258	1 - 4pm (Sun)
Gravesend Chinese School Gravesend, Kent	01474 533093	2.30 - 4.30pm (Sun)
Ying Wah Chinese Language Studies Guildford, Surrey	01483 572293	12 noon - 2pm (Sun)
Portsmouth Chinese Class Portsmouth	01704 267896	1 - 3pm (Sun)
True Jesus Church (Portsmouth) Chinese Class Portsmouth	01234 867420 or 865198	11.30am (Sun)
Southampton Chinese Community Association Chinese School Southampton	01703 771899 or 01831 250778	12.30 - 3pm (Sun)
Chinese Association of Woking Chinese Class Woking, Surrey	01483 222860	10 - 11.30am (Sat)

East Anglia

South East Essex Chinese Essex	01702 469833	1 - 3pm (Sun)
Essex Chinese Class Colchester	01206 871099	1.30 - 3.30pm (Sun)
Harlow Chinese Class Harlow, Essex	01279 508418	11am - 1pm (Sat)
Norfolk Chinese Association Chinese Class Norwich	01603 51630	Sunday

Scotland

Kut O Village Benevolent Society Chinese School Ayrshire	01560 21812	2pm (Sun)
Dundee Chinese School Dundee	01382 452466	2 - 3.30pm (Sun)

CHINESE LIFE IN BRITAIN
149

Directory of Chinese Schools

Name of School and Place	Telephone	Day & hours of opening
Edinburgh Chinese Christian Fellowship Chinese School Edinburgh	0131 361 8393	2.15 - 4.15pm (Sat)
Edinburgh (HK) Chinese Association Chinese School Edinburgh	0131 228 5276	1 - 3pm (Sat)
AI ZHEN Chinese Class Edinburgh	0131 447 6343	10am - 12 noon (Sat) & 2 - 3pm (Sun)
Elgin Chinese Class Elgin	01309 76663	1.30 - 2.30pm (Sat)
Glasgow Chinese Christian Fellowship, Children Fellowship Glasgow	0141 357 2752	11am - 2pm (Sat)
The Glasgow Junior Chinese School Glasgow	0141 443 2444	11am - 3.15pm (Sat)
Perth Chinese School Perth	01738 31222	12 noon - 2pm (Sun)
Stirling Chinese School Stirling	01786 50025 or 50292	1 - 3pm (Sun)

Northern Ireland

N.I. Chinese Chambers of Commerce Chinese School Belfast	01266 656774 or 653931	1 - 3pm (Sun

Index to the main text